# FARMS AND FOODS OF THE GARDEN STATE

## A NEW JERSEY COOKBOOK

# THE HIPPOCRENE COOKBOOK LIBRARY

Afghan Food & Cookery
African Cooking, Best of Regional
Albanian Cooking, Best of
Alps, Cuisines of The
Aprovecho: A Mexican-American Border Cookbook
Argentina Cooks!, Exp. Ed.
Austrian Cuisine, Best of, Exp. Ed.
Bolivian Kitchen, My Mother's
Brazilian Cookery, The Art of
Bulgarian Cooking, Traditional
Burma, Flavors of
Cajun Women, Cooking With
Calabria, Cucina di
Caucasus Mountains, Cuisines of the
Chile, Tasting
Colombian, Secrets of Cooking
Croatian Cooking, Best of, Exp. Ed.
Czech Cooking, Best of, Exp. Ed.
Danube, All Along The, Exp. Ed.
Dutch Cooking, Art of, Exp. Ed.
Egyptian Cooking
Filipino Food, Fine
Finnish Cooking, Best of
French Caribbean Cuisine
French Fashion, Cooking in the (Bilingual)
Germany, Spoonfuls of
Greek Cuisine, The Best of, Exp. Ed.
Gypsy Feast
Haiti, Taste of, Exp. Ed.
Havana Cookbook, Old (Bilingual)
Hungarian Cookbook
Hungarian Cooking, Art of, Rev. Ed.
Icelandic Food & Cookery
India, Flavorful
Indian Spice Kitchen
International Dictionary of Gastronomy
Irish-Style, Feasting Galore
Italian Cuisine, Treasury of (Bilingual)
Japanese Home Cooking
Korean Cuisine, Best of
Laotian Cooking, Simple
Latvia, Taste of

Lithuanian Cooking, Art of
Macau, Taste of
Mexican Culinary Treasures
Middle Eastern Kitchen, The
Mongolian Cooking, Imperial
New Hampshire: From Farm to Kitchen
Norway, Tastes and Tales of
Persian Cooking, Art of
Poland's Gourmet Cuisine
Polish Cooking, Best of, Exp. Ed.
Polish Country Kitchen Cookbook
Polish Cuisine, Treasury of (Bilingual)
Polish Heritage Cookery, Ill. Ed.
Polish Traditions, Old
Portuguese Encounters, Cuisines of
Pyrenees, Tastes of The
Quebec, Taste of
Rhine, All Along The
Romania, Taste of, Exp. Ed.
Russian Cooking, Best of, Exp. Ed.
Scandinavian Cooking, Best of
Scotland, Traditional Food From
Scottish-Irish Pub and Hearth Cookbook
Sephardic Israeli Cuisine
Sicilian Feasts
Slovak Cooking, Best of
Smorgasbord Cooking, Best of
South African Cookery, Traditional
South American Cookery, Art of
South Indian Cooking, Healthy
Sri Lanka, Exotic Tastes of
Swedish, Kitchen
Swiss Cookbook, The
Syria, Taste of
Taiwanese Cuisine, Best of
Thai Cuisine, Best of, Regional
Turkish Cuisine, Taste of
Ukrainian Cuisine, Best of, Exp. Ed.
Uzbek Cooking, Art of
Warsaw Cookbook, Old

# FARMS AND FOODS OF THE GARDEN STATE

## A NEW JERSEY COOKBOOK

### BRIAN YARVIN

HIPPOCRENE BOOKS
NEW YORK

Book and jacket design by Acme Klong Design, Inc.
Photography by Brian Yarvin.

For more information, address:
HIPPOCRENE BOOKS, INC.
171 Madison Avenue
New York, NY 10016

ISBN 0-7818-1083-3
Cataloging-in-Publication Data available from the Library of Congress.
Printed in the United States of America.

# TABLE OF CONTENTS

# ACKNOWLEDGMENTS

A book like this couldn't exist without people who are true believers, because that's what it takes to make a commitment to agriculture in a densely populated and extremely diverse state like New Jersey.

I'd like to thank Karen Anderson and Erich Bremer from the Northeast Organic Farming Association of New Jersey, who began the process of introducing me to the state's farmers. Thanks also to Dr. Tim Jacobsen, Director of the Aquaculture Technology Program at Cumberland County Community College. He's a passionate supporter of farming in a part of the state that's very far from the glitz and glamour of urban fine dining and celebrity-filled markets. Bill Moran of the Whole Earth Center in Princeton also took time out from his very busy routine to help me find the right people.

And the biggest thank you of all to the thirty farmers who opened their doors, fired up their coffee pots, and told their stories. Without them there'd not only be no book, but no food. They play a truly important role in our lives.

Lastly, I must thank my wife Maria, who tasted almost every recipe in this book and listened patiently while I described every detail of every farm visit, right down to the last barking dog. She deserves more appreciation than I can show here.

# INTRODUCTION

When most people close their eyes and try to imagine a New Jersey farm, it's unlikely they'll be able to picture anything other than highways, condos, and shopping malls. Indeed, even (or perhaps especially) long-time residents find it impossible to believe just how much is grown here. There are those New Jersey tomatoes, but people often talk about them in the past tense, unaware that thousands of pounds of locally grown heirloom tomatoes, deep red, bright yellow or zebra striped, are sold in farmer's markets every day during harvest time.

Tomatoes are just the start though. Eggplants and peppers are both huge crops and so are potatoes, beets, zucchini, pumpkins, cabbages, and a whole host of others. Apples, peaches, pears, and strawberries are all fruit that thrive here. New Jersey is the number two cranberry producer in the United States. Our bogs are a remarkable sight in the Pine Barrens, a landscape that doesn't otherwise look like it could support farming.

In fact, farmer's markets can be found in all parts of the state and in every sort of environment. During the peak growing season, countless roadside stands beckon drivers almost everywhere. Get off the Turnpike at exit 2 and drive towards Mullica Hill or head down Route 23 in Sussex County. You'll find amazing variety. Dozens of towns, including Morristown, Westfield, and Summit, also offer seasonal venues with anywhere from a few to fifteen or so vendors setting up shop at specified times. Farmers also head to the state's big flea markets—Englishtown has a large area devoted to them and Cowtown even sells livestock.

Retail farm stands are an important part of the New Jersey rural scene. "There's something about going to these places. It's a personal thing, even if it's just a guy by the side of the road, people will stop," says Abe, the manager of the Lafayette Farmer's Market in Sussex County. Jonathan White, the owner of Bobolink Dairy, comments, "Small scale and progressive agricultures are growing here. We can't compete with Agribusiness, thank god!" Dairies produce cheeses from both cow's and sheep's milk that rival any in the world. Free-range eggs that can be chosen one by one, meats that include buffalo, goat, venison, organic beef and pork, heritage breeds of poultry, and even fish farms that produce oysters, tilapia, and trout are all part of the state's bounty.

Living on the dividing line between rural and urban puts these people in a unique situation. They thrive by growing items too fragile or expensive for most of the rest of the country to even consider. Heirloom tomatoes and doughnut peaches can be brought to market within hours of being picked and handmade cheeses can be priced at levels that approach the best Manhattan gourmet food stores and still sell briskly. Even lettuce at twelve dollars a pound is snatched up with enthusiasm.

Farmers have embraced the challenge. How can they tempt the market? What can they grow that will excite chefs, consumers, and food fanatics? Heirloom eggplants? Rare strains of Italian cattle?

Herbs in a hundred varieties? This thinking breeds even more ideas: cultivated clams and oysters? Fine wines? Sheep's milk cheeses?

On a map of the United States, New Jersey looks pretty small. Wedged in between New York and Pennsylvania, it seems like there isn't much room for anything. But a drive from Duttonville, at the northernmost corner, to Cape May, the most southerly point, is over two hundred miles and takes you through every imaginable environment short of a desert.

In the north, farmers work in an area reminiscent of West Virginia with low, steep mountains and rocky soil. In the center of the state, the landscape becomes more gentle and the farms almost seem like they're in Ohio or Indiana. South of Trenton, the land becomes flatter and you'll find the Pine Barrens—an area with little agriculture except for cranberry bogs. Below them, farms are much larger and holdings of hundreds of acres are common. Down here, the city loses its influence and wholesale-oriented farms dominate. You'll see hundreds of acres of eggplant followed by thousands of acres of peaches and blueberries. At the southern tip, in Cape May, the sandy soil blends into the seashore, perfect for aquaculture.

Meanwhile, real estate developers covet every last square inch of this area. Farms are lost to warehouses, factories, townhouse developments, convenience stores, strip malls, office complexes, chain restaurants, and well, the list goes on and on. Day by day, the population of New Jersey and the amount of space each person occupies keeps growing.

New Jersey farmers are fighters. This is the country life, with fields of vegetables, grazing livestock, and orchards full of fruit. But this is also the suburban life, with a Starbucks, a stockbroker, and a shopping mall right down the road. New Jersey farmers are not just out there in the country; they are a visible part of local culture. Greeting you at community farmer's markets, quoted in the newspaper, and even chatting with celebrity chefs on TV and radio, they are key players in our food universe.

While this book is about what people grow, it's also about what people eat. Because of its huge and varied immigrant population, New Jersey's residents prepare a wider range of dishes than just about any other place on Earth. Vegetable curries? Stewed kimchee? Clam chowder? You'll find them all here.

The New Jersey farm isn't the pastoral sort of place a farm in Vermont or Wisconsin might be, but it's a very real reflection of the state it resides in—a crossroads of every aspect of the American experience.

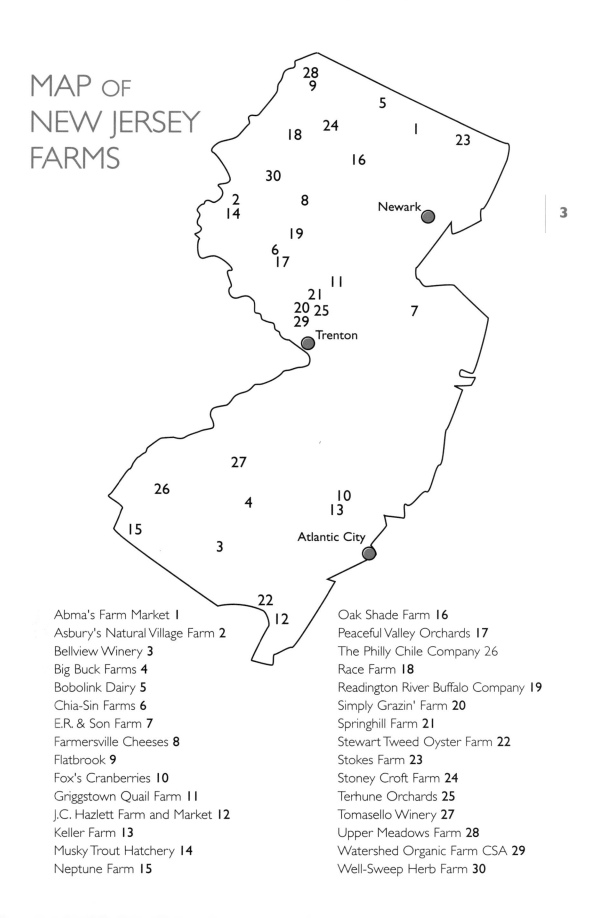

# MAP OF NEW JERSEY FARMS

28
9
5
18
24
1
23
16
30
2
14
8
Newark
3
19
6
17
11
21
20 25
7
29
Trenton
27
26
4
10
13
15
Atlantic City
3
22
12

Abma's Farm Market 1
Asbury's Natural Village Farm 2
Bellview Winery 3
Big Buck Farms 4
Bobolink Dairy 5
Chia-Sin Farms 6
E.R. & Son Farm 7
Farmersville Cheeses 8
Flatbrook 9
Fox's Cranberries 10
Griggstown Quail Farm 11
J.C. Hazlett Farm and Market 12
Keller Farm 13
Musky Trout Hatchery 14
Neptune Farm 15

Oak Shade Farm 16
Peaceful Valley Orchards 17
The Philly Chile Company 26
Race Farm 18
Readington River Buffalo Company 19
Simply Grazin' Farm 20
Springhill Farm 21
Stewart Tweed Oyster Farm 22
Stokes Farm 23
Stoney Croft Farm 24
Terhune Orchards 25
Tomasello Winery 27
Upper Meadows Farm 28
Watershed Organic Farm CSA 29
Well-Sweep Herb Farm 30

# WINE AND CHEESE

# WINE AND CHEESE

It seems like America discovered both wine and cheese in the late seventies. Before that, wine was something that foreigners made with their bare feet (remember that episode of "I Love Lucy"?) and cheese was a gloppy substance that melted over bread and burgers. We all thought cheese with paper between the slices was the height of luxury. But one day, something happened—Brie showed up. It was smelly, had a strange sort of crust, it oozed—and people ate it with great enthusiasm.

By the early eighties, we consumed wine and cheese to show that we knew something. We were popping the corks of French and Italian bottles with vigor and trying every cheese—rind and all—we could get our hands on. Our culinary world grew, and suddenly there was cheese from Norway and Holland and even Swiss from the actual country of Switzerland.

It wasn't a big jump from Italian wine to California wine. In the minds of many New Jersey residents, they were roughly the same distance away and equally foreign. Wines from other parts of the country began showing up too. Oregon, Washington, and the Finger Lakes Region of New York soon had bottles in local stores and the world of American wine exploded.

New Jersey farmers were slower to notice of this explosion. Descendants of the Italian immigrants who'd been in the area for generations continued to make wine on a small scale and provide milk and curds for makers of fresh cheese in urban areas as if nothing had happened. During the past few years, however, a new generation of cheesemakers has set up shop in the state with herds of cows, goats, and sheep. And those winemakers, with their old family recipes and local grapes, have suddenly found a broad new audience.

Of course, all this great wine and cheese brings up a big question: What do you do with it? People seem comfortable trying new and different wines, but those cheeses really look scary. Covered with mold, reeking of strange odors, and looking for all the world like something you'd work hard to avoid, they represent a new frontier for many American consumers.

"The question I get asked the most," says cheese guru Jonathan White of Bobolink Dairy, "is 'Can I eat the rind?'" Of course, within seconds of saying this an intern calls out, "In some cheese, the rind is the best part!" Jonathan assures us that he always eats the rind, "but you don't have to."

An amazing piece of cheese and an equally remarkable slice of bread (and Jonathan makes both) are all some people need. But for special occasions, an arranged cheese platter can make the event. Paul Pappas of Summit Cheese Shop in Summit, New Jersey says, "A great cheese plate needs a variety of tastes and textures. I like to pair things from Italy or Spain with a local cheese." This gives diners a chance to experience the range of flavors that a type of cheese can offer.

The pairing of wine and cheese doesn't have a set of rules. Make matching wine and cheese an ongoing adventure. The wine and cheesemakers in New Jersey are tireless experimenters. There are always new grape varieties and new cheesemaking techniques and these create more possibilities. How about a wine made from native New Jersey grapes served with a local cheese?

The classic, strongly flavored cheeses from Bobolink Dairy and Farmersville Cheeses go well with many of the local whites including Bellview's lettizza or chardonnay and Tomasello's Atlantic County traminette, rkatsiteli and chardonnays. Another great match with artisanal cheeses is Bellview's port, a local rendition of an old classic.

These cheeses also pair really well with berry wines, rapidly becoming a Garden State specialty. These are more like light, fruit liqueurs than wines and provide a rich contrast to the unctuousness of the cheese. Try Tomasello's blackberry, red raspberry and blueberry wines — all classic examples of the genre. Bellview's cranberry, blueberry and starlight blues are also great examples.

Paul continues, "Passion is the biggest word." If you get the chance to meet these wine- and cheesemakers, that passion will overwhelm you. Pay them a visit, taste their wares, and enjoy the fruits of their labor.

# Sangria

YIELDS 10 CUPS

Every Saturday night, the classic Spanish fruit and wine beverage is mixed up in homes and restaurants all over the state. About the only things these drinks have in common are the name and the promise that a secret ingredient makes that particular sangria better than every other. This sangria combines the revealed secret ingredients of at least four different hosts and can work its special magic in several ways: Not only can it make a party festive, it makes even the fiercest of fruit refusers reconsider and gives everybody their daily serving of red wine.

**6 cups red wine***
**I cup brandy**
**I cup Triple Sec**
**I cup *limoncello* (Italian lemon liqueur)**
**2 tablespoons honey**
**I apple, peach, or pear, cored or pitted and chopped (about I cup)**

Mix the wine, brandy, Triple Sec, and *limoncello* together. Put in the fruit—it will float to the top—and chill thoroughly. Serve it well chilled to avoid watering it down with ice. Make sure each drinker gets a few fruit pieces.

* Try this recipe with one of New Jersey's fruity red wines, like Bellview's Homestead or Tomasello's Cape May Red. If you can't get them, and light red wine will do.

# Tomasello Winery

If you were to say that regional wineries have been springing up all over America, Jack Tomasello of Tomasello Winery would agree with you. Indeed, he might even be willing to admit that this trend has affected New Jersey. But there's one thing you could never argue—that his winery has been part of this boom. Tomasello was around when "New Jersey wine" meant Italian-American immigrant families making it for their neighbors. They were producing wine before most Americans drank it, and they continue today, when being a local grower and winemaker is beginning to have some cachet.

While some of the land that makes up Tomasello Winery has been in the family for four generations, it wasn't always a vineyard. Before 1933, Frank Tomasello, Jack's grandfather, raised peaches and raspberries. But when the repeal of Prohibition came, he saw a window of opportunity. With one of the first post-Prohibition wine producer licenses issued in New Jersey, he put in grapes and started making wine, offering half-gallon and gallon jugs. Soon his son Charles was old enough to help out, and things haven't stopped growing since.

Today, Tomasello Winery has thirty-nine wines on their tasting list, starting with Atlantic County Ranier Red, moving on to their versions of the European classics like chardonnay, pinot grigio, and cabernet sauvignon, along with native grape varieties like niagara and ives, and ending with Atlantic County Stuben. Jack says, "Our vineyard reminds me of the U.N. because we have grapes from all over the world and we're continuing to experiment and bring in new kinds."

Walk around Tomasello Winery and you'll notice one important thing—they make lots of wine here. In fact, they're the largest producer in the state, making more than 50,000 cases in a good year. Spend some time in the tasting room too, and see how many different kinds there are. The Tomasellos are the sort of winemakers who are willing to try anything and it's here that their efforts are on display. People have been known to spend a half hour on sparkling whites alone.

So what do these wines taste like? Is it even possible to describe what they offer without resorting to the sort of wine writing that South Jersey farmers aren't likely to take seriously in the first place? Reports from wine buffs tell a story that could have been scripted by any fresh fruit and vegetable fan; the wines grown from native grapes are both the most interesting and the best values.

Also worth noting are their fruit wines. Today, wine made from blueberries, cranberries, raspberries, and strawberries are a novelty, but back in colonial America, wine made from all sorts of fruit as part of daily life. Tomasello's fruit wines have a way of reminding you of basic food memories. Their cranberry wine is reminiscent of cranberry sauce and the blueberry has the distinct sweet spiciness of a great slice of blueberry pie. Both of these wines are made from fruit produced by the Tomasello's neighbors in Atlantic County.

With seventy acres of grapes, Tomasello Winery is tiny by Atlantic County standards and huge compared to many other small retail farms. In fact, with six tasting rooms, 600 retail outlets, and fruit-wine distribution in Taiwan, Korea, and Japan, they have a greater reach than any other New Jersey winery.

You might think that all this is enough for one family, but there's more: At Tomasello's winemaking facility on Route 30 in Hammonton, they run "The Vintner's Room," a catering hall with its own staff of professional chefs. They do weddings, banquets and special wine dinners with private-label bottling as an important feature of the event.

All over the state, the wine business is growing dramatically and Tomasello is one of the main engines of that growth. Active experimentation, tasting rooms, and aggressive marketing, give people in New Jersey a good reason to take local wine seriously.

# Polenta

4 SERVINGS

When the men of Bellview Winery (page 14) describe them- **1 cup cornmeal**
selves as coming from the "corn eating part of Italy," they don't **½ teaspoon salt**
mean corn on the cob. They are talking about polenta, the
boiled cornmeal dish that replaces pasta in the northern part of Italy. This is the dish to try when
you can't look at pasta or potatoes one more time and you need something to go with a toma-
to- or brown sauce-based dish.

Combine the cornmeal with 1 cup cold water and stir until smooth. Let it stand for 5 minutes. Bring 2 cups of water to a boil in a medium saucepan and add the salt. Now add the
cornmeal mixture to the boiling water and simmer over medium heat for 5 minutes, stirring frequently. With big, slow-forming bubbles, it will look like something out of a cartoon. After 5 minutes, the mixture will be fairly thick. Lower the heat, and cook for 20 to 25 more minutes, until
the mixture is smooth and thick. Turn off the stove and let it stand 5 minutes more. It's now
ready to serve.

# Chicken Liver Risotto

4 SERVINGS

This recipe was inspired by the people at Bellview Winery. It combines a classic risotto with chicken livers, a traditional ingredient.

**4 cups chicken broth**
**1 cup dry white wine***
**2 strips bacon, finely chopped**
**1 medium onion, finely chopped (about 1 cup)**
**3 cloves garlic, finely chopped**
**1½ cups white or brown arborio rice (other short-grained rice can be used in a pinch)**
**8 ounces chicken livers, coarsely chopped**
**Salt**
**Freshly ground black pepper**

**H**eat the broth and wine in a saucepan and keep warm.

Put the bacon in a large saucepan and cook over medium heat until it begins to brown and crisp. Add the onion and garlic and stir occasionally, until the onion is translucent. Now put the rice and chicken livers in the pan and cook, stirring for another minute. Add 1 cup of the wine mixture, stirring until the liquid is absorbed. Then add another cup of liquid and stir until it's absorbed. At this point, lower the heat so the rice mixture doesn't scorch, but don't stop stirring!

Continue adding liquid 1 cup at a time, stirring, until the rice becomes soft and creamy (about 20 minutes for white rice or 45 for brown). If you run out of liquid before this happens, use warm water. Season with salt and pepper to taste and serve immediately!

* Try Bellview's Viognier or Niagara.

# Bellview
# Winery

Landisville, ATLANTIC COUNTY

As you head deeper and deeper into southern New Jersey, you notice the scenery start to change. Suburban homes and malls are fewer and the land becomes flatter. Farms change too. Small properties with a few cows and a vegetable patch give way to larger single crop operations.

In the northern part of the state, many of the farmers are people who grew up in the city or suburbs and chose to return to the land as an adult. Not so down south. Farms are more likely to be in the same family for generations and tradition plays a very important role in daily life. Joe, Jim, and Lee Quarella, the father, son and grandson who run Bellview Winery in Landisville are one such farm family. Since the first Quarella arrived from Italy in 1905, there has been winemaking here.

Bellview Farms is 150 acres on the edge of the Pine Barrens. This is the sort of place whose location is hard to describe. It's roughly between Philadelphia and Atlantic City and far from any highway. In the Quarella family for five generations, the farm was woods when they bought it and they cleared a little bit at a time. The first Bellview crop was turnips, grown between the stumps during those first years.

Unlike their colleagues in North Jersey, the Quarellas have never been to a retail farmer's market. In fact, wine is their first try at selling to the general public. At a fancy food show at the Garden State Convention Center, the crowd was a bit skeptical, but was won over by how easy their wines—especially their fruity dessert wines—are to drink. Down on the farm, you'll see something few wine experts could ever imagine—local New Jerseyites stopping by their neighborhood vineyard to buy a bottle or two of as if it were the most normal thing in the world.

In the recent past, they did contract produce farming, growing Chinese vegetables for specialty markets, but Jim remembers, "Something deep down said this was a good place to grow grapes." He was always interested in wine, and with a BS in horticulture he was well prepared to understand the craft's intricacies. Finding a bottle or two made by his great-great-aunt Ada buried in the farm's dusty cellar didn't hurt either. It reminded him of the tradition of gastronomic excellence that the family has always nurtured.

Grandpa Joe continued along a similar theme, talking about how they and their neighbors maintained traditions from the far north of Italy. "Our ancestors were corn eaters," he tells me. "They
ate polenta with brown sauce or red." Indeed, they even ate leftover polenta for breakfast. After
further questioning, it turns out that the "brown sauce" he was talking about was nothing like
modern northern Italian sauces, but instead was thickened with butter in a classic country-French
method.

The Quarella family tree also has a branch from the rice producing Le Marche region—a part of
Italy almost unknown to Americans. When asked what his favorite rice dish is, Joe announces, "pig's
liver risotto" without missing a beat. This is obviously a dish that pre-dates current food aesthet-
ics. When he sees people cringe, Joe suggests substituting chicken livers (as the recipe on page 13
does), but Jim and Lee immediately disagree.

The tales of Italian cooking don't stop there. Hen soup, sardines for breakfast, homemade
salamis…this segues into a general discussion of how South Jersey farmers ate long ago. "As the
crops came in, that's what we ate," beginning with broccoli rabe and ending with cabbage from
the cellar. There was also lots of hunting and fishing to supplement the family cows and pigs. The
Quarella family made butter and simple cheese too.

Today, Jim is the master chef of the household and both Joe and Lee can't stop raving about his
food, but what about the wines? He was looking for a new challenge and the winemaking aspect
of it appealed to him. "It was a whole new art to learn." He also saw the potential for local markets, and as it turns out, his customers are almost all within an easy drive of the farm.

Although he had grown wine grapes all along as a hobby, Jim made the move to commercial production in 2000 with three acres. His vine plantings have grown steadily, and this year he's up to
twenty-two. Lee shows off the vines: merlot, cabernet franc, syrah, lemberger, viognier, chardonnay, cabernet sauvignon, cayuga, ives, pinot grigio, and niagara. Dessert and fruit wines are a
strength here and cranberry, blueberry, and raspberry wines really stand out.

Returning to the winery building, there are rows of barrels and tanks filled with wine. As if somebody was wondering, Joe remarks, "Any parties we have, we make sure we have enough
wine…and we have a lot of parties."

# Baked Artichoke and Cheese Custard

4 SERVINGS

This is one of few dishes in this book that encourages you to use frozen vegetables. You may be lucky enough to get 2 cups of fresh artichoke hearts, but odds are, most of us will reach for the freezer. The frozen artichoke hearts available in most supermarkets will do the job just fine.

Preheat the oven to 325°F and grease 4 (16-ounce) ramekins.

Blend the artichokes, milk, and garlic in a food processor. The mixture need not be completely puréed, but should resemble a thick milkshake. Pour the mixture into a bowl and add the cheese, egg whites, eggs, seasoning, salt, and pepper and mix thoroughly.

Now put the artichoke mixture into the prepared ramekins and place them in a large baking pan. Fill that pan about an inch deep with water—this is called a bain-marie, and it will help the custard cook evenly. Put this whole rig in the oven and bake for 2 hours, until the tops are nicely browned. Serve quickly while still warm. They will fall if left standing too long.

6 to 8 large fresh or 8 ounces frozen artichoke hearts
1½ cups milk
2 cloves garlic
1 cup (4 ounces) shredded cheddar or colby cheese
3 large egg whites
2 large eggs
1 tablespoon Italian seasoning
1 teaspoon salt
1 teaspoon ground white pepper

# Bobolink
# Dairy

Vernon, SUSSEX COUNTY

How many times have you looked at a container of milk and a piece of cheese and wondered how one became the other? Or even worse, how that milk could become either a Kraft Single or a tub of grated Parmesan?

Bobolink Dairy in Vernon makes its own cheeses from its own milk, bakes remarkable bread, and is a place where you can have your food and farm questions answered. It's run by Jonathan White, a cheesemaking guru, nicknamed "The Curd Nerd": Listen to him talk about cheesemaking, bread baking, or Tibetan yaks, and you'll get the feeling that you're in class with a beloved college professor. Walking through the barn at milking time, Jonathan will expound on bovine personalities. He'll pat one of his twenty milking cows on the head and say, "Cows are klutzes with horns!" Soon he'll be on to milk and milk handling: "The more you to do it, the worse it gets," he'll exclaim.

Back in the cheese room, he may mention a recent TV appearance on "Emeril," or he may just talk about conventional wisdom in the dairy business, declare that it's "often wrong," and start describing one or another of his many innovations, such as precision electronic controls and unique cross-breeds of cattle.

On any given weekend, you can find Jonathan presiding over tastings outside his barn/cheese-making room or next to the outdoor wood-burning bread oven. Watch him take a loaf's temperature to see his passion in action. When you visit, make a point of meeting those "klutzes with horns," the cows that make this whole thing work. There are guernseys, Ayrshires, Dutch belted, and jersey/holstein crosses right now, but as Jonathan develops his herd, he's moving towards an Ayrshire/guernsey mix. They really do love grazing on the

farm's roughly 200 acres. A farmhand says, "Even in the winter, even when it's snowing, the cows don't mind sleeping outside."

If you're squeamish, you might be put off by the way mold covers all the cheeses offered for tasting. But this is just part of the natural process and these molds are an important part of the cheese's flavor. When Jonathan brings out a huge, mold-covered Lebanon bologna (handmade by a cheesemaking Amish family and given to him as a gift) you may be a bit startled, but here, everything is in its unprocessed form.

Jonathan and his helpers make these cheeses in a room that's in the same barn as the cows. The milk is put in a vat where it's stirred and warmed to the correct temperature, then rennet—the substance that curdles milk in cheesemaking—is added, and bits of solid white stuff appear in the milk. Soon the tub is so full of those cheese curds that they can be strained off and pressed into molds. Next, the molds are weighed down and left to drain a while longer. At that point, the cheeses are removed from the molds and put in the storage "cave" (which is really just another room in the barn). It sounds easy, but is filled with the sorts of intricate details of temperature, time, texture and technique that transform a simple farm chore into an art form.

Tasting the cheeses on the farm, surrounded by the sights and smells of the dairy, is a sensory experience that's not to be missed. From softer cheeses like Fallen Pyramid to hard ones like their Cave-Ripened Cheddar, they explode with a rainbow of flavors: salty, sweet, earthy, and unctuous. Indeed, his tasting room might be one of the happiest places in New Jersey.

# Chile Cheese Corn Muffins

12 MUFFINS

Muffins like these can be served as a spicy party snack or as a side dish. Make them in advance and freeze them so they can be quickly warmed up when they're needed.

Preheat the oven to 400°F and grease a muffin pan.

Mix the cornmeal, flour, and baking powder together and sift them into a bowl. Slowly add the milk, egg, salt, and oil and blend. Now add the cheese, chiles, oregano, and cumin and mix well. Pour into the prepared muffin pans—the cups should be no more than two-thirds full—and bake for 30 minutes, until springy and light brown. Cool a few moments before serving or cool completely and freeze until needed.

1 cup cornmeal
1 cup all-purpose flour
1 tablespoon baking powder
1½ cups milk
1 large egg, beaten
½ teaspoon salt or garlic salt
2 tablespoons olive oil
1 cup (4 ounces) shredded cheddar or colby cheese
1 tablespoon crushed chiles
1 tablespoon dried oregano
½ teaspoon ground cumin

# Potato Pizza

4 SERVINGS

This is the sort of Italian home cooking that never seems to make it into restaurants. The concept is simple; you make a crust from thin slices of potato and then top it as you would a regular pizza. Potato Pizza is also the perfect dish to try if you want to use a mandoline or other vegetable slicer. The recipe here is for a white pizza with mushrooms, but use your creativity to make other combinations.

1 pound Yukon Gold potatoes, thinly sliced
1 teaspoon salt
1 teaspoon freshly ground black pepper
2 ounces chopped mushrooms (about 1 cup )
1 cup (4 ounces) shredded mozzarella cheese
2 tablespoons fresh rosemary

Preheat the oven to 350°F. Brush a 9 x 13-inch baking sheet with olive oil and arrange several layers of potato slices to form a crust. Season with the salt and pepper and bake for 25 minutes. Remove the potatoes from the oven and evenly cover with the mushrooms, cheese, and rosemary. Return to the oven for 20 more minutes, or until the cheese begins to brown. Cool slightly and serve.

# Stoney Croft Farm

Lafayette is a pleasant enough country town with a small outlet mall, antique shops, and a café. Route 15, a major thoroughfare between New York City and the Poconos, runs right through it. But there is also a maze of roads that starts in town and quickly becomes rural. This land is green with rolling hills and small streams. From clearings and high ground, you can look west and see mountains in the distance, in every other direction, there are rolling hills, farms and suburban homes.

Just a mile from town, there are patches of woods, a checkerboard of farms, and an occasional suburban-style house. It is here you'll find Stoney Croft Farm, the home of Ken and Julie Bechtold and their fourteen jersey cows.

Ken came to Stoney Croft Farm twenty-eight years ago, and Julie followed soon after. When she got there, they had pigs, sheep, and chickens, but their beautiful green pastures cried out for cows. As the herd grew, so did their milk supply. They had to do something with it and that something was cheese. With a cheesemaking textbook and a ready supply of raw material, they were on their way.

The Bechtolds produce several hundred pounds of colby and cheddar cheese a week and sell it both at their farm and at local markets in Montclair and Morristown. Ken is the sort of guy who always has fire in his eyes. He is ready to stand up for the little guy and is not just a farmer, but also a food buyer's advocate. Some Stoney Croft cheeses cost less than the major brands in local supermarkets. Unlike those brands however, they are made from milk with no chemical additives, hormones, or antibiotics. Moreover, you can phone Ken and Julie and be fairly certain one of them will answer. "Anybody who's selling cheese for those prices is really overcharging in my book. I know what the milk is worth!" he asserts and, "This is not a cheese you would serve at a fancy party. We want people to use it in their daily diet."

Ken is the idealist, and Julie is the pragmatic one. Julie is typically up early making cheddar. For over an hour, she rakes the curds and regularly takes their temperature. During this time, she talks about her "girls," the Stoney Croft cows. "We try to keep the cows happy: the happier the cows, the richer the milk," Julie notes. She never lets her attention drift away from the task at hand: cows, milk, cheese. In the barn, New Age music plays and she explains, "Low stress equals happy cows!"

Today, Julie's girls, the fourteen milking cows, look pretty happy. They form a closed herd. All the cows were born on the farm—an important step in maintaining their health.

"A happy cow makes good cheese," is the Bechtolds' mantra. Even though there isn't much to graze on in the dead of winter, a nice stroll in the cold air does them good.

Ken boasts of their health, "We don't need a vet, our cows don't get sick." His cows are under a vet's supervision, but this statement is his way of reminding me that they don't need all those drugs and supplements.

On a cold February morning, Julie stands outdoors with a tall glass of iced tea—half tea and half cubes in twenty-three degree weather. She smiles and says, "Country people are hearty people."

# Macaroni
# and Cheese

4 SERVINGS

Today, many people don't even realize that macaroni and cheese can be homemade. It's so closely associated with boxes and frozen products that we forget its roots. However, it's an American classic and thousands of recipes have been carefully handed down over the generations. This one is fairly typical and a perfect vehicle for Stoney Croft Farm's cheddar cheese.

8 ounces elbow macaroni
1 cup milk or half-and-half
1 egg, lightly beaten
1 teaspoon Italian seasoning
1½ teaspoons salt
¼ teaspoon freshly ground
　　black pepper
2 cups (about 6 ounces)
　　shredded cheddar cheese
½ cup (about 2 ounces)
　　grated Parmesan cheese
1 cup green peas*
1 large bell pepper, cut in strips

Preheat the oven to 350°F. Grease a 9 × 13-inch baking dish.

Cook the pasta for 1 minute less than the package indicates. Drain the macaroni, rinse it in cold water, and drain it again.

Combine the milk, egg, seasoning, salt, and pepper in a bowl and mix well. Add the cheddar and Parmesan to the milk mixture and make sure all the cheese is thoroughly coated. Mix in the cooked macaroni, peas, and peppers. Pour this mixture into the prepared baking dish. Bake for about 1 hour, or until the top begins to brown. Stir the mixture in the pan about every 20 minutes so it doesn't burn.

* In the dead of winter when this dish is most appealing, don't be afraid to use frozen peas.

# Onion Soup

4 SERVINGS

One of the biggest differences between restaurant cooking and home cooking is time. A chef will take the extra moments required to make sure that meats are perfectly browned or beans are properly soaked. This recipe demonstrates that some time on the stove can transform ingredients as basic as onions into something really special.

The Bechtolds' colby or cheddar (page 21) is perfect for this recipe, but don't hesitate to experiment.

1 tablespoon olive oil
4 medium-size onions, 2 of them
   chopped (about 2 cups)
   and 2 of them thinly sliced
1 teaspoon salt
1 teaspoon freshly ground
   black pepper
½ teaspoon dried thyme
4 cups chicken or beef broth
Shredded cheese

Heat the oil in a heavy pot over medium heat. Add the chopped onions, salt, pepper, and thyme. Stir occasionally, until the onions become a brown paste. This will take 40 minutes to 1 hour.

Add the sliced onions and cook until they are soft and translucent. Keep stirring. Add the broth and simmer for 15 minutes, making sure the chopped onions disintegrate in the liquid. Meanwhile, preheat the oven to 400°F.

Put the finished soup in single-serving ovenproof ramekins and cover each one with a layer of cheese. Put the ramekins in the oven for about 5 minutes, or until the cheese melts and just begins to brown.

# Farmersville Cheeses

Califon, HUNTERDON COUNTY

Eran Walswol, the shepherd, salesman, cheesemaker, janitor, truck driver, and cellarmaster for Farmersville Cheeses is one of the toughest people to locate in New Jersey agriculture. He could be at the Union Square Greenmarket in New York City, but maybe not. Farmersville Cheeses doesn't produce enough for him to sell there every week, so he only comes to every other market. He makes appearances at other markets too; his favorite is in Bernardsville. "It's small and wonderful…people buy more cheese in three hours than most markets sell in a day in a rare marriage of money and taste," he notes.

Eran could easily sell every last crumb of Farmersville cheeses to fine restaurants and cheese shops, but that wouldn't be as entertaining as going out and schmoozing with fellow farmers, offering tastes to customers, and generally trying to convince urban consumers that sheep do indeed produce milk and that it can be turned into really delicious cheese. Eran is obsessed with a sheep cheese ideal—a firm, aged product with a depth of character and earthy flavor that just won't come from any other animal.

Where else can you look for Eran if you need to find him? At the site of his new farm in Long Valley, supervising the building of what is destined to become one of the largest sheep dairies in the region, or in various government offices obtaining the myriad permits required to bring 900 animals to live and work in a spot less than sixty miles from America's largest city.

Of course, Eran also spends time with his flock, 130 strong on twenty acres in the heart of central New Jersey. And in his cheese room and cellar, conveniently close to those sheep. He is with them for their two milkings a day and he's the one that feeds them when they can't graze in the dead of winter.

Eran appears to be a heavyset middle-aged man in overalls. But within minutes, he'll strip off his top layer, revealing a trim man who happens to be wearing two sets of clothes. He explains that to make life easier, he always wears his cheese-making outfit under his farmer's garb.

A person is unlikely to develop a lifelong passion for sheep cheese growing up in New Jersey, but Eran Walswol was born in Israel and raised in Belgium. "The greatest cheeses come from Belgian Abbeys," he says. "It's because of the ages of molds that have gathered on the walls of the caves." But life brought him to New Jersey and handed him a career building high-rises in Hoboken.

Eran is married and has two children, so he isn't completely alone at Farmersville Cheeses. He met his wife Debbie at Steven Institute of Technology, where they both earned degrees in engineering. She handles most of the paperwork for the farm. Chelsea, his teenage daughter, works right alongside her father. She milks, helps in the cheese room and cave and pretty much runs market stands by herself. "I walk away and she handles it," Eran boasts. Ethan, his son, is younger and helps too, but isn't quite ready to make the commitment his sister has.

Talking about the cheese business in general, Eran says that it seems like there's no limit to the amount he can sell. In fact, he'd like to see increased competition, so the industry as a whole would attract more attention. "More cheesemakers would create more interest." He continues, "Cheese should be sold on quality, not myth. What I try to make is an international quality cheese. I am the happiest when visitors from Europe buy my cheese because it reminds them of what they have at home."

Eran sees four different levels of cheese production: industrial made in giant factories; cooperatives, where a large group of farmer members band together in the hope of producing something a bit better than industrial (Cabot in Vermont for example); artisanal, where a small shop buys milk from one or two known producers; and the smallest—farmsteads like his own or his good friends at Stoney Croft Farm and Bobolink Dairy.

These categories help explain one of the biggest questions that face New Jersey cheesemakers: pricing. The artisans charge more than the famous imports, but those big names are almost never handcrafted in the same way. Small farm, handmade, European cheeses are hard enough to find in Europe. What you see that's brought here is almost always from cooperatives or small factories, a different item at a different price.

For Farmersville Cheeses, the most important thing is the quality of their product. There is no way they could exist without a total commitment to excellence. As Eran carefully examines each aging wheel of cheese, he says, "If you don't add value, it's just a hobby."

# FISH AND SHELLFISH

# FISH AND SHELLFISH

Who'd have thought? Most of us know that salmon is farmed north of New Jersey and catfish is raised down south, but what fish grow here? Tilapia for one. Students at Cumberland County College and inmates at Bayside State Prison raise it and there are several other small commercial operations. Musky Trout Hatchery has been offering trout for almost 150 years. And down near the Delaware Bay, oyster farmers have become more active as coastal areas are cleaned up and the water becomes purer.

In a sense, these are the early days of fish farming in New Jersey, but aquaculture facilities are going in all over the state. People are raising not only tilapia and trout but also striped bass and other fish. As Cumberland County College graduates more specialists and the demand for fish keeps increasing, you can be sure that there will be producers to meet this need.

# Pickled Oysters

4 SERVINGS

**30**

Don't let anybody tell you that oysters have to be fried or smothered in butter and cream to be eaten cooked. This dish lets the oysters shine through without the addition of anything rich. Don't forget to allow time for it to marinate before serving!

In a pot or double boiler, warm the oysters over low heat with 1 cup water until they're cooked through—less than 1 minute. Remove the oysters from the cooking liquid and set them aside. Add the peppers, vinegar, peppercorns, bay leaves, allspice, and salt to the liquid and bring it to a boil. Cook for 1 minute. Lower the heat to a simmer and cook, stirring occasionally, for about 15 minutes, until the flavors have combined. Cool the mixture and add the oysters. Let stand in the refrigerator for at least 8 hours before serving.

1 pint shucked oysters, including the liquid
2 small chile peppers
2 tablespoons cider vinegar
1 tablespoon whole black peppercorns
2 bay leaves
1 tablespoon whole allspice
½ teaspoon salt

# Stewart Tweed
# Oyster Farm

Green Creek, CAPE MAY COUNTY

If you really don't want to be noticed, pick an occupation that most people aren't aware of, then locate yourself at the end of a sandy road behind a campground. Finally, make sure your facility is out of sight and can be approached only by those wearing rubber boots or hip waders.

This is the case with Stewart Tweed and his oyster beds. Who even knew that oysters grew on farms? Who would think of looking for such a farm behind a campground that is hidden behind a trailer park? To make matters worse, it's located on the shores of Delaware Bay, that no-man's-land part of New Jersey, below the Pine Barrens and between the Turnpike and the Garden State Parkway. But quiet roads, fishing piers, and great bird watching all make this area worth visiting. Inexpensive farm stands and modest seafood restaurants that dot the back roads seal the deal.

Oyster farming has a long history in New Jersey. Most of the early beds were in places that may once have been pristine seashore, but haven't been in the past couple of hundred years. Before the Civil War, for example, Bayonne was home to a large oyster fishery.

Stewart Tweed's is a working farm, but it's also a beach. There is sand, driftwood, and dune grasses. Look down and you'll see baby horseshoe crabs scurrying around. Visiting in the early fall, you'll find brilliant sun and a rich blue sky. It's the sort of place that feels like you should be drinking beer and throwing a Frisbee. But Stewart and his son James—who farms the neighboring beds—see this as their workplace.

With a large beard and knee-high galoshes, Stewart Tweed looks like a very intelligent Santa Claus—a Santa who loves oysters. When asked about what drew him to this work, he says, "Oysters are much nicer than clams because they are individual and gregarious." He holds up a baby (called a "spat" in oysterman jargon) to demonstrate his point and shoots his listeners a sly smile — no creature of the land or sea is less gregarious than an oyster.

"They are a species that defines a habitat," he continues. When oysters flourish in a place, it tells you that the ecosystem there is thriving. And these oysters are said to be incredibly good, partially because of the high levels of plankton at Stewart Tweed's, but also because of the Tweeds' skill. "We're trying to take science and apply it." Stewart is a former State Marine Extension Agent who did graduate study in shellfish and James grew up at his father's side. These guys *really* know their oysters.

For the non-oyster farmer, the most amazing thing about this operation is that oysters eat nothing but the plankton suspended in seawater. That's right—no feed, no antibiotics, and no hormones—just seawater, and very clean seawater to be sure. They do need a couple of years on the beds to mature, but the rest is almost free. There isn't much equipment needed either: mesh plastic bags to hold the oysters, the wooden pier-like beds they sit on, and small plastic drums called "hats" that the baby oysters incubate on. The land—underwater land of course—is made available from the state through a riparian grant for about a dollar an acre a year.

To an untrained eye, Tweed's farm looks like a bit of driftwood or a long-deserted pier being lapped up by the waves of the Delaware Bay. But Stewart sees things differently. For him, his oysters are fascinating and his property isn't really even that remote. He thinks it should be easy to find, saying, "Just look for the abandoned plastic cactus by the side of the road."

# Oyster Pancakes

4 SERVINGS

Oyster pancakes take all sorts of forms in the Garden State. There is the western kind made with traditional pancake batter and Asian versions: Chinese- and Japanese-style with wheat or made the Korean way with rice flour. Why do we use a mix here? Because it's what the oyster farmers themselves use. You can substitute a good buckwheat pancake recipe if you prefer.

1 pint shucked oysters, chopped
½ cup chopped scallions (green parts only)
½ teaspoon salt
½ teaspoon ground white pepper
3 cups prepared buckwheat pancake batter
Butter or oil for cooking

**33**

Mix the oysters, scallions, salt, and pepper into the pancake batter and make sure they're evenly distributed.

Put a bit of butter or oil in a skillet over medium-high heat. Pour ½ cup of batter into the pan and let it cook until you see bubbles around the edges, about 2 minutes. Turn it over with a spatula and let it cook for another minute, or until both sides are nicely browned. Serve them right from the pan with a good hot sauce. They can be kept warm for a little while in a low oven, but don't wait too long or the oysters will tougher.

# Manhattan-Style Oyster Chowder

6 SERVINGS

South Jersey oyster farmers eat oysters in only a handful of ways: in a milk based stew, in pancakes, raw, breaded and fried, or as oysters "Rockefeller." Didn't anybody make them in a tomato-based soup or chowder? Nobody had ever heard of it. It was a challenge that couldn't be resisted.

Put the bacon, garlic, oil, chile pepper, and seasoning in a 6-quart pot over medium heat. Cook, stirring until the bacon starts to brown and the garlic becomes translucent. Add the onion and potato and continue cooking, stirring occasionally, until the potatoes and onions are tender. Now add the tomatoes and liquid, salt, and pepper and simmer, uncovered, for about 15 minutes. Add the oysters—liquid and all—to the pot and give it a few stirs. Serve immediately or the oysters will toughen.

2 slices thick-cut bacon, diced
2 cloves garlic, minced
1 tablespoon olive oil
1 dried chile pepper, crumbled
1 teaspoon Italian seasoning
1 medium onion, diced (about 1 cup)
1 medium russet or Yukon Gold potato, diced (about 1 cup)
1 (28-ounce) can diced plum tomatoes, including the liquid
1 teaspoon salt
½ teaspoon freshly ground black pepper
12 shucked oysters (1 pint), including the liquid

# Mikado Salad

4 SERVINGS

Older books on haute cuisine occasionally refer to a "Mikado Salad" and describe it as a combination of rice and oysters. Such a dish seems like a wonderful appetizer or addition to a buffet table, but it doesn't appear in any modern cookbook. What to do? Update the old one of course!

Bring a medium pot of salted water to a boil. Put the bell peppers, peas, and carrots in the pot and cook them for 1 minute. Add the oysters and cook for 30 seconds more. Be careful not to overcook them or they will become tough. Cool the oyster/vegetable mixture by pouring it into a serving bowl. Toss it with the rice, vinegar, oil, salt, and pepper. Let stand for 30 minutes before serving.

½ bell pepper, cut into strips
¼ cup fresh or frozen green peas
1 small carrot, peeled and chopped (about ¼ cup)
1 pint shucked oysters, drained
2 cups cooked basmati rice
2 tablespoons white wine vinegar
2 tablespoons walnut oil
1 teaspoon salt, plus extra for blanching
1 teaspoon ground white pepper

35

# Musky Trout Hatchery

Just past exit 6 on I-78, north of the town of Bloomsbury, lies some of the most pastoral and untouched land in the state. Here, along the banks of the Musconetcong River, Vern Mancini and his son Jeff run the Musky Trout Hatchery, the only commercial trout farm in New Jersey.

The Musky Trout Hatchery has a long and varied history. One of the oldest hatcheries in the United States and certainly the oldest in New Jersey, it was established in the early 1860s by Dr. J. H. Slack, an early aquaculture pioneer. It ran on a small scale until the 1940s, when it was briefly abandoned. Vern took the place over in 1958 with the intention of opening a hunting and fishing store, but the demand turned out to be for trout and that's what they concentrated on.

Trout are picky animals. They expect perfection: clean water at the correct temperature and a specific feed. All are provided at Musky. With a 1,200 gallon a minute dedicated spring putting out water at 51°F year-round and an automatic on-demand feeding system, every trout need is satisfied. The water is fed into a series of ten holding ponds, each protected by netting from the trout's major predators, osprey and blue heron. Vern says that while these birds may be endangered in the world at large, they are plentiful where trout congregate.

Five varieties of trout are raised at the trout hatchery: rainbow, brown, tiger, brook and golden, along with large-mouth bass, minnows, and warm-water fish for decorative ponds. At any given time, there are about 100,000 mature trout in the outdoor ponds and about 500,000 fry (as newly hatched trout are called) in the indoor hatchery. Currently, the operation is completely self-contained.

Vern and Jeff strip the eggs from the females—it looks like they're milking them—and obtain the reproductive milt from males in the same way. In the earliest stage, the trout look like tiny golden specks in the smallest of the indoor hatchery ponds. This gold is the egg's yolk sac. After a few weeks, they begin to look like fish, and not long after that, they're moved outside.

Asked for more details, Vern hands over a reprint of an article that appeared in the June 13, 1868 issue of *Harper's Weekly*. This piece describes the hatchery and its activities as if it were written yesterday. Only the names of the owners have changed.

Vern's office is a cross between a rustic hunting lodge and a library, with mounted trophy fish on some walls and an amazing assortment of old aquaculture textbooks lining the others. Most notable is a hand-bound copy of the earliest American book on the subject, *Practical Trout Culture* by J.H. Slack, MD, written in the 1860s at this very property.

In the dark, cool hatching room, there is all sorts of sensory stimulation: the rushing water of the spring, and the sounds of mature fish jumping in the ponds. One thing is missing though: Wherever you go at the Musky Trout Hatchery, you won't smell fish. Instead, there's the fragrance of the crisp air of western New Jersey farm country.

Trout farming isn't something you do for instant gratification. It takes at least a year to take a trout from egg to market and the fish are carefully sorted by age and size. The smallest look like the tiny dried shrimp you see in Asian shops and the largest could be mistaken for salmon. There is market demand for all sizes. Smaller fish are used for decorative ponds, larger ones for stocking fishing ponds or eating, and the biggest have had modeling careers on popular cooking shows.

When people think of farming, they tend to imagine corn, tomatoes, or pigs, but trout are as much a crop as any of these. Droughts, floods, diseases, freak storms, early frosts, and late heat waves are all perils that demand worry. As Vern says, "It's a constant struggle with the elements."

# Gefilte Fish

4 SERVINGS

When the Jewish holidays come around, people all of a sudden start talking about gefilte fish. They buy it in cans and jars, and even sometimes from delis, but they rarely make it from scratch. And no wonder! Most recipes call for fish that are rarely offered in modern markets and in quantities so huge that handling them becomes impractical.

Just what is gefilte fish? Gefilte fish means "stuffed fish" in Yiddish. Ages ago, a stuffing of fish, eggs, bread crumbs, carrots, celery, and onions was crammed into a whole fish skin and served sliced. Somewhere and somehow, this dish morphed into the boiled dumpling we know today. Traditional gefilte fish recipes call for whitefish or carp, but you can substitute easier to find fish like trout and tilapia, both farm raised here in New Jersey. This dish is normally served cool with horseradish sauce, but it is fantastic (and in a way a whole different dish) straight from the pot.

**TO MAKE THE POACHING LIQUID:** Combine the fish broth, 4 cups water, the wine, onion, carrot, and celery in a soup pot and bring it to a boil. Boil for 1 minute. Reduce the heat to a simmer and cook, covered, for 1 hour, stirring occasionally.

## POACHING LIQUID

- 4 cups fish broth
- 1 cup white wine
- 1 medium onion, quartered
- 2 carrots, peeled and cut into large chunks
- 2 celery stalks, cut into large chunks

## FISH DUMPLINGS

- 2 pounds fish fillets, skinned and cut into large pieces
- 1 celery stalk, finely chopped
- 1 medium carrot, peeled and finely chopped (about ½ cup)
- ¼ cup dry bread crumbs or matzo meal
- 1 egg
- 1 teaspoon salt
- ½ teaspoon freshly ground black pepper

**TO MAKE THE DUMPLINGS:** Place the fish, celery, and carrot in the food processor and process until they form a paste. Put the mixture into a bowl and add the bread crumbs, egg, salt, and pepper. Mix thoroughly and let stand for 10 minutes. If you made the broth ahead of time, bring it back to a simmer and mold the fish mixture into 1-inch balls. Simmer the dumplings in the broth, covered, for 10 minutes stirring occasionally, until they are firm to the touch. You may have to do this in batches. Remove the dumplings from the pot and place them in a large bowl. Strain the broth and pour it over the bowl of dumplings. Serve chilled with shredded horseradish.

# Trout Baked in White Wine and Herbs

2 SERVINGS

Is there a way to cook a trout besides steaming or frying? This method is simple and requires little active preparation.

Preheat the oven to 325°F.

Combine the broth, wine, garlic, peppercorns, oregano, thyme, cilantro, and bay leaves in a baking dish large enough to hold the fish. Give the ingredients a good stir and lay the whole fish in the liquid.

Cover the pan with foil and bake it for 1 hour, until the fish flakes easily.

2 cups fish broth
2 cups white wine
1 head of garlic, unpeeled, but cut in half
1 teaspoon whole black peppercorns
½ teaspoon dried oregano
½ teaspoon dried thyme
½ teaspoon dried cilantro
2 bay leaves
2 (24-ounce) whole trout, cleaned

# Trout Baked in Parchment Paper

1 SERVING

This simple method is one that at first seems strange, but does a really great job of retaining flavors without added fat. You can buy food-grade parchment paper in supermarkets and kitchen supply stores. You can also use aluminum foil; they even sell foil bags for this purpose, but they're expensive and don't seem to retain flavors the same way parchment does.

½ cup coarsely chopped broccoli
½ cup coarsely chopped carrots
1 whole (1-pound) trout, cleaned
1 teaspoon salt
1 teaspoon freshly ground black pepper

Preheat the oven to 350°F.

Microwave the broccoli and carrots on high for 2 minutes, or until they're about half cooked.

Take a sheet of parchment paper, about 24 inches long and fold it in half. Put the paper on a baking sheet and lay the trout out on one of the halves. (You may need to remove the head and tail). Mound the broccoli and carrots in small piles next to the fish and season with salt and pepper. Crimp the paper using a series of small folds, to seal the fish and vegetables inside. Bake the package for 30 minutes, until the fish and vegetables are completely cooked.

**NOTE:** Some people seal the parchment packages with staples. Resist the temptation. The danger of burns from the hot metal or worse, somebody ingesting a staple, is just too great.

# Russian-Style Fish Pie (*Pirok*)

6 SERVINGS

In Russian, *pirok* means "pie," and fish pies are quite popular. This is a perfect cook-ahead meal or a dish that can be used for potlucks or packed lunches. It works with all sorts of fish: tilapia, trout, whiting, or in a pinch, canned salmon.

Preheat the oven to 350°F.

Sauté the onion in the butter in a medium pan over low heat, until translucent. Add the salt and pepper. Add the chopped fish and rice. Mix thoroughly, add the beaten egg, and remove the pan from the heat.

Fit the bottom piecrust into a 9-inch pie pan. Put the fish mixture in the crust, cover with a second crust, and bake for 1 hour, or until the crust is golden brown. Cool for 10 minutes before slicing and serving.

1 medium onion, chopped
   (about 1 cup)
1 tablespoon butter
1 teaspoon salt
1 teaspoon ground white pepper
16 ounces chopped fish fillet
   (about 2 cups)
2 cups cooked rice
1 lightly beaten egg
1 double batch piecrust dough
   (see page 193)

# POULTRY AND EGGS

# POULTRY AND EGGS

Chicken is a sort of lightning rod. We Americans eat so much of it that we should think about what it was fed and what went into producing it. Yes, chicken can come from a factory, but it can also be raised on a small family farm. Eggs can be harvested from a coop with 60,000 hens or a small shed housing just ten or fifteen. This is all good news for chicken and egg fans.

Fresh eggs are something you'll find at almost every farmer's market. They're relatively easy to farm and attract the consumers' attention. These eggs represent a level of quality that most of our great-grandparents took for granted. With rich yolks and intense flavor, they add a new dimension to egg dishes. Try them in an omelet, a custard, or just fried in butter, sunny-side up.

Free-range chicken offers us the same sort of revelation. Birds sold as stewing chickens don't fall apart in the pot, fryers are tender and juicy, and all are raised in an environment that you can often examine yourself. Prepare a pot of Coq au Vin (page 55) or bake Chicken Pot Pie (page 58) and enjoy the difference.

In addition to chicken and eggs, New Jersey farmers raise turkeys, quails, pheasants, and other birds. All will reward the adventurous cook.

# Cranberry-Roasted Chicken

2 TO 3 SERVINGS

In Italy, people traditionally put a lemon and some herbs in the cavity of a chicken when they roast it. This burst of acidity and citrus gives the bird a remarkable jolt of goodness. But lemons aren't the only acidic fruit. Cranberries do the job too and with an unusual flavor twist of their own.

**1 (2½- to 3-pound) roasting chicken**
**Salt**
**Freshly ground black pepper**
**½ cup fresh cranberries**
**2 (3-inch) sprigs fresh rosemary**

Preheat the oven to 350°F.

Wash the chicken inside and out and pat dry with paper towels. Check the inside of the cavity carefully. Make sure there's nothing left in there! Season the inside with salt and pepper. Place the cranberries and rosemary in the cavity. Close the opening with one of those great clips sold for just this purpose (purists can truss it with butcher's twine). Season the outside with more salt and pepper. Put the bird on a rack in a roasting pan and slide the whole thing into the oven. Cook for about 2 hours, or until a meat thermometer inserted in the thigh reads 180°F. Let the chicken rest for 10 or 15 minutes before carving and serving.

# Soy-Braised Chicken

4 SERVINGS

One of the most enduring sights in New Jersey's Chinese communities is those braised chickens and ducks that hang in the windows of many shops and restaurants. You see them in noodle shop windows and at the takeout counters in Asian mega-grocery stores. Served with rice and greens on the side, they make a favorite quick meal. To many people, these chickens are as frightening as they are delicious. How are they made? Can they really be prepared at home? Read on:

1 cup soy sauce
¼ cup packed brown sugar
¼ cup dry sherry
1 head garlic, unpeeled, but cut in half
2 tablespoons honey
3 (¼-inch thick) slices fresh ginger
1 tablespoon five-spice powder
1 (3-pound) chicken, well rinsed

In a pot large enough to hold the chicken, combine the soy sauce, sugar, sherry, garlic, honey, ginger, and five-spice powder with 1 cup water and bring to a boil, stirring occasionally. Reduce the heat and simmer for 10 minutes. Add the chicken, and cook, covered for 25 minutes, basting frequently. Flip the chicken and simmer, basting for another 25 minutes, until cooked through. Remove the chicken from the pot and let cool to room temperature before serving.

# Flatbrook
# Farm

Flatbrook Farm is the sort of place that people dream of when they want to get out of the city. There are open fields, rolling hills, and beautiful red barns. This is the country! On a chilly February day, snow blankets the pastures and makes the wooden fences between them look like they are sketched in with pencil. Silos, wood-framed farmhouses, and animals nibbling on winter feed complete the picture.

With 400 acres spread out over the northwest corner of Sussex County, the property is perfect for grazing, and at any given time, there are cows, goats, and 500 chickens, all enjoying the pleasure of strolling, eating, and being part of a pastoral landscape. When spring comes, turkeys raised for the holiday season join in a lively, scene that could be right out of a children's book.

Days here revolve around the feeding and care of the animals. Making sure there is enough food and water is the job of Bob Campbell, the resident farmer and the man who took Flatbrook from modest production to its present state as one of the region's leading organic meat producers.

In a place like this, you can really see the animals exhibit their instinctive behaviors. Goats and cows are curious and chickens really do display a pecking order. An alpha female rules the hens and roosters fight it out for top honors. Bob never ceases to be amazed at how they create their own social structure. Cows, goats, and chickens all clearly know exactly where they stand.

Before Bob, a single elderly farm hand worked the land here. But even then, the property owners, a well-to-do family from Manhattan, insisted that he never use chemicals. This made organic certification easy. Their location, with one of the farm's pastures facing the main road between New York City and the Poconos, gives them plenty of exposure to passing traffic. This turned out to be a great tool for marketing.

Rustic signs that say, "Naturally Grown Lean Beef" and "Pasture Raised Chicken and Turkey" beckon from Route 206. You can follow them to smaller ones that read, "Farm Store" and they'll lead you off the main road and over to Flatbrook's market. People stop in on their way to weekend homes in Pennsylvania and they return to stock up when they head back to the city.

What do they come for? Beef of course, whole and cut up chickens, and beautiful free-range eggs. With a bit of advance planning, you can also purchase what Bob calls "freezer meats," larger quantities at lower prices. And during the holiday season, their free-range organic turkeys are available too. Goat fans should know that Flatbrook Farm is the only organic producer in New Jersey. You can buy butchered meat in the store or whole animals for halal slaughter.

With all this remarkable food at his disposal, Bob insists that his favorite thing is a hamburger. He loves burgers made from his own animals and cooked over a wood fire out in the yard. But wherever he is, that's what he'll go for. Out with his wife and family, the rest of them could be having lobster, fine pastas, and wine and Bob will be sitting with that burger. When asked if any burgers he's had out were as good as his own, he was polite enough to decline to answer.

Even without chemicals or industrial farming techniques, Flatbrook Farm is totally sustainable. The owners have several goals: to maintain it as a beautiful place, to preserve the qualities of life that the farm contributes to the area, and to continue producing fine organic meats and making them available in the community. Bob and succeeding generations of Flatbrook farmers are in it for the long haul.

# Chicken Stuffed with Fried Rice

2 TO 3 SERVINGS

Some people are obsessed with takeout food. They seem to feel that those cardboard and plastic containers convey some sort of magic, that somehow this food is superior to what's either in the freezer case or even worse—their home. This dish uses one of the most basic takeout items as a main ingredient. It's an homage to everybody who's stood at one of those counters with a paper menu and a pencil.

Preheat the oven to 350°F.

1 (2 to 3 pound) roasting chicken
1 pint fried rice from your local Chinese takeout restaurant
½ cup Chinese barbecue sauce*

Rinse the chicken inside and out and pat dry. Examine the cavity and make sure that there's nothing left inside. Stuff the cavity with the fried rice and close with a clamp or kitchen twine.

Brush the sauce on the chicken skin, making sure the whole surface is covered with a thin even coat. Put the chicken on a rack in a roasting pan and place in the oven. After about 1 hour, check for doneness with a meat thermometer. When you get a temperature of 180°F at the thigh and the juices are clear, it's ready. Let it rest for 10 minutes at room temperature before serving.

* Chinese barbecue sauce can be found in the Asian section of your local supermarket, but always available at a much lower price in a Chinese grocery.

# Spice-Rubbed Roast Chicken

4 SERVINGS

Dry rubs are a seasoning technique that is popular in the southern and barbecue cooking tradi-tions. They give a unique depth of flavor. One word of warning though: Do not buy the spices listed here in those little plastic bottles in the supermarket. If you do, this will be the most expensive thing you ever cook. Stores that carry bulk spices will sell them for a tiny fraction of the price. See the Glossary (page 195) and shopping guide (page 203) for suggestions.

Combine the sugar, paprika, cumin, chili powder, mustard, garlic salt, seasoning, and salt in a bowl.

Preheat the oven to 425°F. Grease a baking sheet.

Dredge the chicken parts in the spice mixture and make sure they're evenly coated. Let stand in the refrigerator for 5 to 10 minutes. Place them on the prepared baking sheet and bake for 40 minutes, until the skin has turned golden brown. Let them rest for a moment before serving.

2 tablespoons packed brown or raw sugar
2 tablespoons paprika
1 tablespoon ground cumin
1 tablespoon ground chili powder
1 tablespoon mustard powder
1 tablespoon garlic salt
1 tablespoon Italian seasoning
1 tablespoon salt
1½ to 2 pounds chicken parts with the skin on (thighs work well)

# Abma's Farm Market

Wyckoff, BERGEN COUNTY

In theory, the idea of a farm in Wyckoff isn't quite as strange as the idea of a farm in downtown Newark or the parking lot of the Woodbridge Mall, but you'd never believe it if you were in your car and a couple of miles away. Stop in the nearby Starbucks, and it's filled with blond guys sitting at their laptops and high school kids worrying about their SATs. This is the kind of place that was supposed to have said good-bye to its last farm thirty years ago, but Abma's is still there. Abma's isn't just surviving, it's going strong.

To get to Abma's, you drive up a typical suburban street, cross a railroad track, and suddenly, there's a farm! (And a factory on the other side of the street.) How can a family farm survive in a neighborhood whose main crop seems to have been lawn clippings since before Richard Nixon was president? Easy! Abma's is a destination. Anybody who sets foot in the place is treated to a tour de force of farm stand marketing. If you go and bring your children to the petting zoo, you might also pick up some freshly baked cookies. If you buy tomatoes, you might also buy eggs.

In the store, Abma's own chicken, vegetables, fruit, and baked goods are mixed in with carefully selected items brought in from the outside. Big bins of whatever is currently in season are set out front too. But you don't go to Abma's instead of going to the deli; you go there because it's a real farm in the heart of very suburban Bergen County.

Four generations of Abma's have lived here. Jim, was born on the farm and so were his son and grandson. His father was an immigrant from Holland who bought the place during the depression. They started selling produce in 1950 and converted the old chicken barn into a store in 1971.

That barn was built in the eighteenth century and Jim is very concerned with preserving its history. "We try to keep it authentic. There used to be a bunch of these barns around and this is the only one left," he says. But that barn is now the center of the Abma retail operation, which includes the farm, greenhouses, and a zoo.

Jim Abma is a man with very demanding taste. He rhapsodizes about rural France and makes it very clear that few places in New Jersey meet his standards. He starts naming locations and menus and we talk about classic French dishes like coq au vin and cassoulet. From field to table, Jim takes food very seriously.

**POULTRY AND EGGS**

Jim recounts what he saw as a horror story: Somebody invited him for dinner and served him salad greens from a bag! He says this in a tone that most people would reserve for muggings or embezzlements. There was rage written all over his face.

This was a great insight. He could easily have a top-notch retail gourmet store and abandon the farm operation entirely, but his own demanding tastes require him to keep growing. "I want fresh stuff in the store and I'd rather have my own," he says decisively. He is most proud of his lettuces: chicory, escarole, and a long list of red and green leaf varieties. But he also grows great peppers, and talks about his tomatoes as if they are his children.

Abma's is also in the chicken and egg business. In the store there are whole and cut up free-range birds and baskets of eggs only a few hours out of the nest. Serious egg fans will be delighted to see that not only can they choose them by type and size, but they can also be chosen one by one. So if an egg buyer wants four small browns, three large whites, and two small whites, they can buy what they wish.

The store is a refuge for those serious about seasonal produce and great poultry. Abma's Farm Market really is what so many city stores pretend to be—a place where a someone who loves great ingredients grows and sells them. At Abma's, there's Jim and his thirty acres out back, really growing what's in the store and ready to answer questions from anybody who asks.

More than anything else, Jim Abma is a believer. He believes in himself, his family, and the quality of his products. But Jim believes even more in God. He speaks about how the farm has been hit by floods, frosts, and heat waves and always endures. When the bad comes, he says his prayers, waits a bit, and soon things begin to change. He intones, "Nobody but nobody depends on God in the same way as the farmer."

# Chicken Stewed in Red Wine (Coq au Vin)

4 SERVINGS

Poultry farmer Jim Abma's great chicken and enthusiasm for classic French dishes inspired this recipe. *Coq au Vin*—chicken stewed in red wine—seemed to be the way to go. This dish is based on a recipe from a French home cook. He assures us that we can make this at home after work and not wind up eating at midnight.

Heat the oil in a large Dutch oven or soup pot over medium heat. Season the chicken pieces with salt and pepper and brown them in the oil. Remove them from the pot and add the bacon. When it starts to brown, add the mushrooms, onions, and garlic. Continue to cook the mixture until the onions are translucent. At that point, add the wine and rosemary, return the chicken to the pot, and bring the mixture to a boil. Lower the heat to a simmer and cook, covered, for 40 minutes, or until the chicken is tender.

**VARIATION:** Add 1 pound of small new potatoes when you add the chicken for a one-pot meal.

* Try Homestead from Bellview Winery or American Merlot from Tomasello.

2 tablespoons olive oil
1 (3- to 4-pound) chicken, cut into serving pieces
2 teaspoons salt
1 teaspoon freshly ground black pepper
2 strips bacon, cut into ½-inch pieces
8 ounces small mushrooms (2 cups)
1 medium onion, chopped (about 1 cup)
4 cloves garlic, chopped
1 (750-milliliter) bottle red table wine*
2 sprigs fresh rosemary

# Chicken and Eggplant with Black Bean Sauce

2 SERVINGS

A simple Chinese-style recipe that can be served as part of an Asian meal with rice.

Heat the oil in a large skillet over medium heat. Add the black bean sauce and onion, and cook until the onion is translucent and evenly coated with the sauce. Turn the heat up to high and add the chicken. Cook, stirring until it starts to brown. Add the eggplant and continue stirring over high heat for another minute. Bring the mixture down to a simmer and cook for another 20 minutes or until the eggplant is tender.

2 tablespoons vegetable oil
2 teaspoons black bean garlic sauce
1 medium onion, chopped (about 1 cup)
8 ounces boneless chicken thighs or breasts, cut into bite-size pieces
1 large eggplant, cubed (about 2 cups)

# Chicken Vindaloo

4 SERVINGS

New Jersey's huge Indian community ensures that this classic Indian curry shows up on menus all over the state. Its name comes from its key ingredients vinegar and potatoes, which are called *aloo* in India. Think of this as both a recipe and a basic cooking method. Once you've made it with chicken, the substitution possibilities include, lamb, beef, shrimp or even vegetables like eggplant.

Put the oil and curry paste in a large skillet over low heat and stir until they're combined. Turn the heat up to medium and add the onion. When the onions are translucent, add the chicken and keep cooking until the onions are browned, about 10 minutes. Stir in the tomatoes and potatoes over medium heat. After everything is well coated with the curry mixture, add the vinegar and ½ cup water and lower the heat to a simmer. Cook, covered, for 15 minutes, then remove the lid and cook for 20 or 30 minutes more—until the potatoes are tender.

- 1 tablespoon vegetable oil
- 3 tablespoons vindaloo curry paste
- 1 medium onion, chopped (about 1 cup)
- 1 pound boneless chicken, chopped into large chunks
- 3 medium tomatoes, chopped (about 2 cups)
- 3 medium red potatoes, cubed (about 2 cups)
- ½ cup cider vinegar
- 1 teaspoon salt

# Chicken Pot Pie

6 TO 8 SERVINGS

The humble chicken pot pie has many variations across the state. In some places, it has a New England-style double crust, and down in Salem County, it includes noodles, the way it's made across the Delaware River in Pennsylvania. This recipe is for a real pie though—it can even be sliced.

Preheat the oven to 400°F.

Fit half of the crust in the bottom of a 9-inch pie pan. Toss the chicken, mushrooms, bell peppers, carrots, peas, parsley, salt, and pepper together until they are well mixed and put them in the pie pan. Cover with the top crust, cut some slits in the top to let the steam out, and bake for 1 hour, or until the crust is golden brown. Cool slightly and serve.

1 double batch piecrust dough (see page 193)
1 pound boneless chicken, cut into bite-size pieces (about 2 cups)
4 ounces mushrooms, chopped (about 1 cup)
1 bell pepper, chopped (about 1 cup)
1 medium carrot, peeled and chopped (about ½ cup)
½ cup fresh or frozen green peas
½ cup chopped fresh parsley
1 teaspoon salt
1 teaspoon ground white pepper

# Griggstown Quail Farm

Griggstown (Princeton), SOMERSET COUNTY

No part of New Jersey stays hidden without deliberate effort. Developers scour every square inch looking for potential sites for new townhouses and office buildings. So when suddenly the condos stop and farmlands appear, you know somebody must be working hard at farmland preservation. This is certainly the case with the Griggstown Quail Farm. When asked, owner George Rude, says that the town was so anxious to preserve farmland that they wouldn't even consider installing sewers.

Griggstown is not far from Route 27, but is also seemingly in the middle of nowhere. You turn down a side street, drive a mile, and suddenly you're in the country. George and a partner started the place thirty years ago to breed quails for hunters. As it happened, one of them worked at Lutèce, a legendary New York City French restaurant. Soon afterwards, James Beard came to visit, and he urged the chef at the Four Seasons to serve their quail too. They learned that there was much more money in butchered and dressed quails than in live ones.

Things didn't stop there. D'Artagnan, the distributor of fine foods, began handling their line and they became as big time as an eighty-acre farm can be. They rode the crest of the fine-dining boom and shipped quails, pheasants, and several duck varieties to high-end, high-priced restaurants all over the area. But it was what happened after the boom busted that put Griggstown Quail Farm on the map. Without a steady stream of well-heeled customers, they had to develop a whole new clientele and find ways to bring their products to the community.

Today, the farm has has expanded to include mallard and muscovy ducks, pheasants, partridges, poussins, chickens, and several varieties of turkeys, including the Heritage Bourbon Red. D'Artagnan still distributes their products, but they are as often sold in supermarkets or over the Internet as to fine restaurants. The biggest change from the early days of direct-from-the-farm wholesaling is retailing. George calls this "alternative farming." Both through an on-site shop and a stand at the farmer's market in Collingswood, they sell poultry and a wide range of prepared foods directly to the public.

No birds are caged at the Griggstown Quail Farm. Ducks and turkeys can be outdoors twelve months a year. Chickens need to be brought in during really cold weather, and quails can only leave their barn in the summer. The indoor spaces are clean and well lit and have plenty of food and water. There is no feeling of factory farming here at all.

This retail store makes Griggstown one of the first farms in the state to have its own resident chef, putting them once again on the cutting edge of retail agriculture. He not only bakes their famous chicken pot pies and fruit pies, he cooks several varieties of birds at the farm store and bones and butchers many of them too. Coming soon are a line of sides to complement their poultry. These prepared meals and spit-roasted fowl will be locally-grown and produced "home meal replacements."

Wherever George and his son Chip go, they find their fresh poultry and prepared foods in great demand. At the farmer's market in Collingswood last year, they sold more than 2,800 chicken and fruit pies. In one day, customers bought over 100 turkeys. From home cooks who want to use the quail for exotic recipes to non-cooks who want to pop one of their chicken pot pies in the oven, they always have something extraordinary to offer.

George is lucky he owns the farm, because if he didn't, he'd be the biggest customer. He eats their products at almost every meal. Poussin (very young chicken) is his favorite grilled, pan fried, or roasted, but he also finds room for pheasant, duck and chicken. His recipe almost never changes: salt and pepper are his seasonings and the grill and skillet are his main tools.

For George Rude, the Griggstown Quail Farm has been his life's work. Now, with his wife working in the store and his grown son helping at the markets on weekends, the whole family has joined him. When asked if he has any good stories to tell, his reply is quick, " Every day's a story; every day on the farm you learn something different." On the topic of the future, he is even briefer, "I'll die on the farm."

# Poached Turkey Breast

1 TURKEY BREAST; ENOUGH FOR 3 TO 5 SANDWICHES

Everybody has seen turkey breast at the deli counter. It's a solid hunk of meat that can be thinly sliced for sandwiches, but how does it get that way? Why is turkey at the farm a few dollars a pound and six or more in deli form? Poaching, the process of cooking something in liquid maintained below the boiling point, is a great way to prevent meat from getting tough or dry and does a fine job with turkey breast. With all the great turkey we have here, you should be able to prepare your own, save a good amount of money, and know just where your turkey breast was raised and butchered.

Combine the vinegar, beer, garlic, salt, and rosemary in a glass or plastic bowl large enough to hold the turkey. Add the meat and marinate for at least 8 hours in the refrigerator. Turn it in the bowl every couple of hours.

Preheat the oven to 325°F.

Drain and discard the marinade. Put the turkey and broth in a large, shallow pot. Cover and braise for 1 hour, or until a meat thermometer inserted in the turkey reads 180°F. Let the turkey stand for 10 or 15 minutes before slicing.

2 cups cider vinegar
1 (12-ounce) bottle lager beer
2 heads garlic, unpeeled, but cut in half
2 tablespoons coarse salt
4 sprigs fresh rosemary
1 (1½-pound) boneless turkey breast
4 cups chicken broth

# Quail Marinated in Beer

4 SERVINGS

Quails are little birds with big flavor. Purists will just sprinkle salt and pepper on them and throw them on the grill, but a marinade like this one will give the birds a bit of depth and add some interest.

Combine the ale, vinegar, soy sauce, chiles, peppercorns, thyme, and bay leaves in a glass or plastic bowl.

Rinse and dry the quails. Add them to the marinade and refrigerate for at least 2 hours.

When you're ready to start cooking, preheat the oven to 325°F and oil a baking sheet. Lay the quails out on the baking sheet. Sprinkle them with salt and pepper and bake for 40 minutes, or until golden brown Let rest at room temperature for 5 minutes before serving.

* Flying Fish ESB is a great local example.

** "Butterflied" means cutting the birds along their backbone so they can lie flat on a baking sheet or grill. This is most easily done with poultry shears.

1 (12-ounce) can or bottle ale*
1 cup cider vinegar
1 cup soy sauce
2 whole dried chiles, chopped or 1 teaspoon dried chile flakes
2 tablespoons whole black peppercorns
1 teaspoon dried thyme
3 bay leaves
8 quails, butterflied**
1 teaspoon salt
1 teaspoon freshly ground black pepper

# Pheasant Stew

4 SERVINGS

Often, we think of pheasant as a food from another time. You can more easily imagine Queen Victoria eating it than dining on it yourself. It doesn't belong to the world of air travel and high-speed Internet connections. So when it was time to create a recipe, it seemed best to choose one as archaic as the bird itself.

Fry the bacon over medium heat in a large Dutch oven or soup pot. When it starts to brown, add the onion, garlic, butter, cherries, raisins, thyme, salt, pepper, and cloves and continue to cook, stirring until the onions are translucent. Add the pheasant and cook until the meat starts to brown, about 5 minutes. Next add the broth, wine, and brandy, turn up the heat, and bring the mixture to a boil. Once it boils, reduce the heat to a simmer and cook, uncovered, until the liquid thickens—about 1 hour. Serve with potatoes or polenta (page 12).

3 ounces bacon, chopped
  (about ½ cup)
1 medium onion, coarsely
  chopped (about 1 cup)
4 cloves garlic, crushed
2 tablespoons butter
2 tablespoons dried cherries
2 tablespoons raisins or currants
1 teaspoon dried thyme
1 teaspoon salt
½ teaspoon freshly ground black
  pepper
2 whole cloves
1 (3- to 4-pound) pheasant, cut
  into serving pieces (if you can
  get one with the bones
  removed, that's even better)
1 cup chicken broth
1 cup light red wine
½ cup brandy

# Keller
# Farm

Egg Harbor City, ATLANTIC COUNTY

On a clear day, the first sign of Keller Farm is its wind generator cranking out electricity. Then when you pull into the front parking lot, you can check out the solar hot water heater and a substantial photovoltaic array – a huge panel of solar cells tht generate even more power. Keller Farm puts out about 17 kwh a day of its own electricity. There's also an old Ford pickup at the edge of a field and a small wooden roadside stand with a colorful sign that says, "Farm Fresh Produce." Jim Brandt, Jr., the fourth-generation owner, is nothing if not an idealist and his vision is based first and foremost on being good to the earth.

Keller Farm was started by Jim's great-grandfather, George Keller, back in 1925. In those days, most of the farm's business was selling retail at the market in Atlantic City. Because most of what was

sold there was priced in one dollar units (i.e.. tomatoes for a dollar a basket, cabbage at three heads for a dollar, etc.), Jim remembers the peri-od in a very unusual way. During that time, his grandfather took care of all their finances with dollar bills. No matter how much they owed, it was always paid in ones. In fact, Jim speculates that the house itself was bought with them.

Raised by his grandfather (who Jim always refers to as "Pops"), he was taught strong lessons in both farming and frugality. On cold winter days, Pops would put a kerosene heater under the thermostat in order to make the rest of the house cooler and save money on heat. Jim says, "It was quite a wonderful experience for me. I cooked every day. I never minded. I thought that I had freedom because I was responsible. In the end, I came to understand that the way he did things was the easiest way in the long run."

These days, you could pay for your Keller Farm produce with ones, but you'll probably need fives and tens. However, unlike similar outlets up in the northern part of the state, you won't need twenties. Jim Brandt works hard to keep prices reasonable. Organic free-range eggs at three dollars a dozen are about the most extravagant purchase you can make here. They are his own custom breed; an old favorite Rhode Island Red rooster crossed with Golden Red hens. As part of Jim's work with the community, they are hatched by first-graders at a local elementary school.

Each Keller Farm egg is a unique shade of deep brown and their yolks are closer to red than yellow. Most customers demand them this way. Jim says that, "A white egg can taste as good as a brown egg if the chicken is eating good food." But for him, happy customers are almost as important as happy chickens.

Jim has a total of thirteen acres, all under certified organic cultivation. While some of this land is used for chickens, more is used for vegetables. An amazing array of organic produce is grown here, much of it just because it seems interesting to him. For example, mature broccoli rabe is popular with the local community, but by harvesting it as a young shoot, he's created his own take on Asian spring greens.

Leafy vegetables are really important here. The growing season begins when kale is planted and ends when the last broccoli is picked. Arugula is so important that certain customers—described by Jim as "the arugula people"—make the trip to Keller Farms just for it. He also grows more traditional Asian varieties like mizuna, napa cabbage, and tatsoi.

It should go without saying that Keller Farms grows heirloom tomatoes. But unlike many other farmers, Jim frequently changes varieties. "I don't like to plant the same ones year after year. I always have Romas, but otherwise, if it's an open-pollinated heirloom, I'll grow it. He also grows cucumbers and a number of different squashes, but as with the tomatoes, the types he grows can change from one year to the next.

More than anything, Keller Farm is driven by Jim Brandt's passion. He is here farming because it's what he believes in. He generates electricity and heats water with solar and wind power, he has overseen the organic certification of thirteen acres of land, and he has become an important resource for the community. He makes this point clearly by saying, "I didn't want to become an organic farmer because the profit margin was higher. I did it because it was the right thing to do."

# Baked Omelet

4 SERVINGS

Baked omelets are eaten throughout Spain (where they are called *tortillas*) and Italy (where they're known as *frittate*). Hot from the oven, they are a light alternative to a meat course, but are just as often served cold as a bar snack or sandwich filling. They are also a perfect cook-ahead item to put in a bag lunch or enjoy as part of a quick supper.

This dish requires a good nonstick skillet. Many cooks keep one just for notoriously sticky dishes like eggs. If you become a fan of them, you might consider doing the same.

Preheat the oven to 325°F.

Season the potato with salt and pepper and microwave on high for about 8 minutes, or until tender (they can also be spread on a baking sheet and put in the oven at 325°F for 20 minutes).

While the potatoes are cooking, beat the eggs and milk together.

2 medium Yukon Gold potatoes, cubed (about 1 cup)
1 teaspoon salt
½ teaspoon freshly ground black pepper
6 eggs
½ cup whole milk
1 tablespoon olive oil
1 tablespoon Italian seasoning
1 bell pepper, cut into strips (about 1 cup)

Heat the oil in a large nonstick skillet with an ovenproof handle over medium heat. Add the seasoning and give it a few stirs. Then put in the bell peppers and potatoes and season with a bit more salt and pepper. Pour the milk mixture into the pan and stir until the peppers and potatoes are evenly distributed. The eggs will begin to scramble. Take the pan off the heat and put it in the oven for 30 minutes, or until a knife inserted in the center comes out clean.

# Stir-Fried Eggs
# with Tomatoes

4 SERVINGS

In a Chinese restaurant, this is one of those dishes that few people order, because it doesn't sound very Asian. But in restaurants that specialize in home-style Chinese dishes, you'll see it often. With fresh market tomatoes and free-range eggs, it tastes great and is worth a try.

Heat a wok or skillet over high heat. Add the oil and give it a minute to get hot. Carefully put in the carrot, garlic, ginger, and fish sauce and stir. You should see some serious sizzling action. When the garlic starts to brown, add the tomatoes and scallions. This is stir-frying, so keep stirring! After a few minutes, the tomatoes will be cooked. Lower the heat to medium and add the eggs. Stir gently for about 5 more minutes, or until the mixture is fully blended and the eggs are scrambled. Serve as part of a Chinese meal with rice.

2 tablespoons vegetable oil
1 carrot, peeled and grated
3 cloves garlic, finely chopped
2 tablespoons chopped fresh ginger
1 tablespoon fish sauce
2 cups finely chopped fresh tomatoes
4 scallions, chopped
6 eggs, lightly beaten

# Chinese-Style Tea Eggs

12 EGGS

In this recipe, hard-cooked eggs are simmered in a spiced tea. The result is a classic Chinese snack food that's often sold at the takeout counter of the big Asian grocery stores (see the Shopping Guide, page 203). They are a portable protein source with an unusual flavor.

Bring 4 cups water to a boil in a soup pot and add the tea bags, soy sauce, five-spice powder, and cinnamon stick. Boil them for 1 minute, then reduce the heat to a simmer.

Crack the shells of the eggs but do not remove them. (This allows the flavors to penetrate slowly.) Then put the eggs in the simmering liquid and cook for about 1 hour. Remove the eggs from the liquid and cool. Serve as a snack or side dish with rice or other Asian specialties.

**6 black or oolong tea bags**
**½ cup soy sauce**
**3 tablespoons five-spice powder**
**1 cinnamon stick**
**12 hard-cooked eggs**

# Vegetarian Chopped Liver

4 SERVINGS

This egg and mushroom mixture was once a Jewish deli standard. But despite the popularity of vegetarian dishes, this somehow got lost over the years. Give it a try for a party, a sandwich filling, or a starter.

Put 1 tablespoon of the oil, the mushrooms, onions, and peas in a skillet over medium heat and cook, stirring until the onions have browned. Cool for a few moments, then, combine the onion mixture, eggs, remaining 2 tablespoons oil, salt, and pepper in a food processor and process to a coarse paste. Serve as you would chopped liver with bread or crackers.

3 tablespoons olive oil, divided
12 ounces chopped mushrooms
   (3 cups)
2 medium-size onions, chopped
   (about 2 cups)
2 cups fresh or frozen green
   peas
2 hard-cooked eggs
1 teaspoon salt
½ teaspoon freshly ground
   black pepper

# MEAT

# MEAT

Many people want to believe that our meat comes from contented animals raised by friendly farmers. While this is not always the case, in New Jersey, there are farms where livestock graze freely in rolling pastures and get natural, unadulterated feed when winter comes. There is more than just psychological comfort in all of this. Meat raised this way has a richer and more intense flavor that responds well to all sorts of cooking methods. This fresh air and exercise improves animal health too.

For many people, meat makes a meal. It takes a roast for a holiday, a steak on the grill Sunday evening, or a quick burger on a busy weeknight to know that you're having a real dinner and not just eating a snack.

# Pork and Kimchee Stir-Fry

2 SERVINGS

This dish is found in Korean kitchens everywhere. It's a thrill for lovers of spicy food and a good way to incorporate vegetables in the dead of winter. As for the kimchee itself, buy it fresh at any good Korean or Chinese supermarket, it will be packed in a plastic tray or glass jar. Don't use one in a can!

A dd the pork, oil, and soy sauce to a wok or large skillet over high heat. Cook, stirring until the meat is well browned. Reduce the heat to medium-low and add the kimchee. Mix well and cook, stirring occasionally for about 20 minutes, until the meat is cooked through. Remove from the heat, add the sesame oil, and stir. Serve as part of an Asian meal with rice.

8 ounces pork tenderloin, cut
  into small strips
1 tablespoon vegetable oil
1 tablespoon soy sauce
3 cups prepared kimchee
1 teaspoon sesame oil

# Simply Grazin'
# Farm

Hopewell is the epicenter of New Jersey's agricultural revolution. Farmers in the fields surrounding this quiet town are changing the way that the state thinks about food. Just a few miles from Princeton and Lambertville, acre upon acre of organic fields, tilled by people who are absolutely committed to coaxing the finest products from the soil. It is here that Mark Faille, his wife Karen, and his sister Cindy run Simply Grazin' Farm, a place devoted to achieving the ultimate in organic meats. They produce free-range chicken, grass-fed beef, and naturally raised pork.

When they bought the property seven years ago, livestock was the farthest thing from their minds. Like many outsiders, they were seduced by what Mark called "the romance of vegetables." The way consumers are drawn to great looking produce at markets. As the farm became home to Mark, Karen, their two children, and two dogs, they began to notice a huge hole in the New Jersey natural foods business. Their first two cows were a sign pointing towards the future.

For the Failles, one of the toughest parts of getting started was gathering information. They now have well-worn copies of classic organic farming books like "You Can Farm" by Joel Salatin and "Why Grassfed is Best" by Jo Robinson. (updated versions are available from www.eatwild.com) They had hoped for support from the Northeast Organic Farming Association and the people at the county extension office, but in those days, few people believed in the possibility of small-scale meat production. Organic farming was considered in the realm of vegetarian health food fanatics and not something financially sustainable. So they read and read and read some more.

Soon chefs and restaurants began asking questions. They were looking for grass-fed beef and free-range chickens. The chefs impressed Mark immediately because they were seeking quality, not price. They wanted a superior product and he knew it was one he could deliver.

"Food is too cheap!" Mark declares. There is just no way that grass-fed and chemical-free beef can compete in price with the mass-produced stuff. The vast western feedlots make cattle really big, really fast, and keep their costs relatively low. Simply Grazin' can do better though; it can produce meat that tastes superior and is free from hormones and pharmaceuticals. Luckily, in New Jersey, there's a ready and willing public for their products.

The farm looks more like a park for animals than a meat production facility. Their Piedmontese breed cows wander in large fenced-in areas where they enjoy a diet of green New Jersey grass. The meat chickens, Cornish/white rock crosses, are too small to be stopped by the cattle fences and wander at will. They seem to be part of the familyand the Faille children and dog often visit and play with them. Mark raises Dorchester and Hampshire pigs at another location with the same care and attention.

Simply Grazin' is community focused. "I'd rather see our food in the local school lunchroom than on the plate of the mayor of New York City," Mark asserts. In fact, almost all their customers are within fifteen miles of the farm and their restaurant clientele are in Princeton and Hopewell for the most part. Indeed, this is one of the great advantages of farming in New Jersey. You can have a fertile and profitable operation a few minutes drive from a major urban center.

However, Mark makes it clear time after time that he has no interest in the biggest urban market of them all. He even insists that he's never been to New York City, less than ninety minutes away and the prime destination for most of the area's farmers. Nothing is more important to him than keeping the business local. As he says, "Our goal in life is to make folks aware of quality food and to create the best environment for our children."

# Stuffed Bell Peppers

4 SERVINGS

Stuffed peppers are a popular dish in eastern Europe and a great way to show off some of the beautiful bells that appear in the markets.

Preheat the oven to 325°F. Grease a baking sheet.

Combine the bread crumbs and milk in a large bowl and let stand for about 15 minutes. Thoroughly mix in the beef, pork, onion, carrot, oil, paprika, seasoning, salt, pepper, and cumin. It's best to use your hands for this. In fact, it's fun to use your hands for this!

Cut the tops off the bell peppers so that they look like cups with lids. Remove the white pith and seeds from the insides. Now stuff the meat mixture inside the pepper "cups" and place them on the prepared baking sheet. Bake for 90 minutes, or until the meat is cooked through.

½ cup dry bread crumbs
½ cup whole milk
8 ounces ground beef
8 ounces ground pork
1 medium-size onion, chopped (about 1 cup)
1 medium carrot, peeled and chopped (about ½ cup)
3 tablespoons olive oil
1 tablespoon paprika
1 tablespoon Italian seasoning
1 teaspoon salt
1 teaspoon freshly ground black pepper
½ teaspoon ground cumin
4 bell peppers

# Kofta Kebabs

2 SERVINGS

This is that ground meat dish that's on many Mediterranean menus. When it's put on the table in front of you, it looks like just another meatball or burger, but it doesn't taste that way at all. Instead, several unusual spices work to give this dish a very unique flavor. For a real adventure, head to one of New Jersey's Middle Eastern neighborhoods to buy these ingredients (see Nouri's Brothers Shopping Center, page 208).

Preheat a grill to high heat.

Mix the meat, onion, garlic, parsley, cumin, cayenne, sumac, paprika, parsley, salt, and pepper and combine well. Many people use their hands for this. Now add the bread crumbs and once again mix thoroughly. Let it stand for 15 minutes so the bread crumbs can absorb the moisture.

Next form the mixture into balls no bigger than 1 inch across (any larger and they will fall off) and put them on metal skewers. Grill for 5 to 8, minutes turning frequently, until the meat is deeply browned. Serve immediately. These can be served as part of a Middle Eastern meal with couscous and salad, but also are great with the garlic and parsley sauce on page 126.

1 pound ground beef or lamb
1 large onion, grated (about 1 cup)
3 cloves garlic, minced
3 tablespoons finely chopped fresh parsley
1 teaspoon salt
½ teaspoon freshly ground black pepper
1 cup dry bread crumbs
2 teaspoons ground cumin
1 teaspoon cayenne pepper
1 teaspoon ground sumac
½ teaspoon paprika

**NOTE:** While this dish is great cooked over coals, it will also work in a grill pan on top of the stove or baked in a 400°F oven for 25 minutes.

# Swedish Meatballs

YIELDS 25 TO 30 MEATBALLS; 4 SERVINGS

You would be astounded to learn just how many people in New Jersey make Swedish meatballs and even more astounded when you see how many different variations there are. Sometimes, you get the feeling that any meatball could be called by the name, but a "real" Swedish meatball is mild and not cooked in a sauce. No oregano, no tomato. And the preferred cooking method is with butter in a skillet.

Mix the bread crumbs and milk together in a large bowl until they form a paste. Next add the beef, pork, egg, salt, and pepper and mix thoroughly; try using either a potato masher or your hands. Let the mixture stand in the refrigerator for several hours to combine the flavors.

Form ½- to ¾-inch meatballs. Avoid the temptation to make them larger.

¼ cup dry bread crumbs
¼ cup whole milk
1 pound ground beef
4 ounces ground pork
1 large egg
2 teaspoons salt
1 teaspoon ground white pepper
Butter for frying

Melt the butter in a heavy skillet over low heat. Sauté the meatballs in the pan in batches, without crowding. They will cook slowly but let them take their time. Turn them occasionally so they brown evenly and be sure they are cooked all the way through.

Serve as an appetizer or main course.

# Hungarian Goulash (*Gúlyas*)

4 SERVINGS

Many forms of stewed meat are called "Hungarian Goulash," but there is a real thing. *Gulyàs* is a stew of beef and potatoes and/or dumplings (this recipe calls for potatoes) cooked slowly and seasoned with garlic, paprika, and sour cream.

Heat the lard in a stew pot over medium-high heat. Cook the beef, stirring until it is well browned. Add the onion, garlic, paprika, salt, and pepper and stir. Add 4 cups water and bring the whole thing to a boil. After the mixture boils for 1 minute, add the potatoes and sour cream. Lower the heat and simmer, covered, for 1 hour. Then remove the lid and simmer for 30 minutes more. Remember to give it a stir every 5 minutes or so. The dish is ready when the meat is completely tender.

1 tablespoon lard
1 pound stewing beef,
    cut into 1-inch cubes
1 medium-size onion, chopped
    (about 1 cup)
4 cloves garlic, chopped
2 tablespoons paprika
1 teaspoon salt
½ teaspoon freshly ground black
    pepper
3 medium red or Yukon Gold
    potatoes, cubed
3 tablespoons sour cream

# Neptune
# Farm

The town of Salem and the area around it have a historical look that one doesn't expect to find in the heavily developed and redeveloped state of New Jersey. But here, eighteenth-century buildings are common and farmhouses that age can still be what they were built to be: Houses for farmers, not historic recreations or weekend retreats for wealthy urbanites. Neptune Farm, owned by Torrey Reade and Dick McDermott, is just such a place.

Torrey wasn't always a farmer. Years ago, she lived in a Manhattan loft and wanted out, but with a Manhattanite's view of the world, she had a rough time finding property she could afford. After visiting properties in more well-known areas like the Berkshires and Upstate New York, she somehow found a persistent real estate agent from Salem County, New Jersey, a place that she and most of the rest of the outside world had never heard of.

The property she bought was a far cry from her small loft: It had 126 acres—fifty planted with blueberries—and a colonial house. She and Dick have put a decade and a half of effort into restoring it. Their work has paid off. The brick façade and wooden plank interiors are now in perfect condition and a few pieces of period furniture complete the early American farmstead feeling. When you enter Neptune Farm, you're stepping out of the modern world and back into the eighteenth century.

Far from the suburban and big city markets that provide incomes for other New Jersey farmers, Torrey and Dick can't rely on beautiful displays of vegetables and fruit in the way some of their colleagues can. Instead, they've built a two-prong strategy. They skip annual vegetables like zucchini, corn, and pumpkins altogether and stick with perennials like asparagus, as well as organic meats. Lamb is especially appealing. The animals—only a bit larger than German Shepherds—are small and manageable. Quality cuts are sold in quantity to fine restaurants in nearby Wilmington and Philadelphia and households can buy shares of entire butchered animals. There is little competition and year-round income. Neptune Farm sells lambs by the half-animal and beef by the sixth: butchered, packed, frozen, and delivered.

Grazing lambs keep their front lawn properly trimmed and in the distance, cows nibble on hay bales. Lamb and beef have been good choices for them. Watching the baby lambs suckle their mothers, Torrey comments that she doesn't sell them when they're that young. Instead, she waits until they're "obnoxious teenagers" that she's happy to be rid of. "Our slaughterhouse uses the word 'kill;' they don't hide anything." This is the farmer's paradox—they both love the animals and love eating them.

Asparagus and berries are seasonal and most of the crop goes to retail stores in the northern part of the state. Although Torrey is one of the people who began the Salem farmer's market and recruited many of the vendors, Neptune Farms doesn't sell there. The season doesn't begin until after their fruit and vegetables are gone and quantities of meat just don't lend themselves to tailgate marketing.

With urban backgrounds and more than a decade of farming experience, Torrey and Dick have a strong passion for cooking and eating. Salem and Cumberland counties are home to huge mass-production farms staffed by immigrant labor. This has given the region a vast and ever-changing supply of great, inexpensive Mexican restaurants. Dick talks about them in the same way that many people discuss "cheap eats" in urban ethnic neighborhoods, charting their ups and downs and comings and goings.

A strongly agricultural area with the third lowest per capita income in the state, people in Salem County are really aware of where their food comes from. This means there are many thriving local food traditions that may have died out elsewhere. The local Quaker meeting house offers chicken pot pie dinners that use a crustless recipe unique to the area. Greenwich has an asparagus and eggs breakfast and the local fire department holds a muskrat supper. Crabs and oysters are also an important part of the local diet.

Dick and Torrey also have more refined dining interests and rave about meals at fine establishments in Wilmington and Philadelphia. For Dick though, the best dishes are the samples that chefs offer him when he's delivering farm products. "I don't even know what it was, but they handed it to me and it was delicious," is a typical response.

Things are looking good for Neptune Farm. These days, not only do serious restaurants seek out their output, young families alienated by supermarket products and practices are doing the same. They want to know where their meat comes from, and what sort of people raise the animals. For them, Torrey and Dick are comfort indeed.

# Slow-Cooked Lamb Shoulder

4 SERVINGS

This is the perfect recipe to keep you company on a cold, rainy day. Although this dish has a very long cooking time, it requires little preparation or attention and the results are unique. Just make sure you have the nine hours it requires.

Combine the broth, tomatoes, rosemary, and salt in a large Dutch oven or soup pot with a tight fitting lid and add the lamb. Place it in a cold oven and set it at 200°F. Braise for about 9 hours, turning the meat every 2 hours or so. After 5 or 6 hours, the meat will be so tender that you won't be able to flip it over, so at that point just let it go. It is this very long cooking at a low temperature that gives the lamb its unique texture. The meat is so tender that it can be served with a spoon. No knife is needed.

**4 cups beef broth**
**1 (28-ounce) can crushed toma-toes**
**2 sprigs fresh rosemary**
**½ teaspoon salt**
**1 (2-pound) bone-in lamb shoulder**

**N O T E :**  You can also put small potatoes in the pot during the last hour.

# Braised Veal Shoulder

8 TO 10 SERVINGS

A big piece of meat almost seems frightening to those of us who are used to a chicken breast or fish fillet, but for important dinners and festive occasions, nothing else will do. This technique calls for cooking, both on top of the stove and in the oven. Don't clean the pan after you finish browning—the stuff left on the bottom is part of the flavor.

The recipe calls for a boneless veal shoulder, but the technique also works for beef, pork, or even bison. For pork, use the same method, but check the internal temperature with a meat thermometer (it should read 160°F) before serving.

If your butcher has tied the meat with a net or twine, do NOT remove it until cooking is done. Season the meat with salt and pepper. Heat the oil in the Dutch oven or other large pot over medium heat and brown the roast to a golden color. When the browning is complete, remove the roast from the pot and set aside.

Preheat the oven to 325°F.

Return the Dutch oven to the stovetop over low heat. Add the garlic, anchovies, and seasoning and stir until the anchovies disintegrate. Add the onions and cook, stirring until they just start to brown. Add the broth, turn up the heat, and bring the mixture to a boil. Return the roast to the pot, cover, and put the whole thing in the oven. Bake for 3 hours, until the meat is fork-tender. Allow it to rest for at least 10 minutes before serving.

1 (4- to 5-pound) boneless veal shoulder roast
2 teaspoons salt
1 teaspoon freshly ground black pepper
¼ cup olive oil
6 cloves garlic, chopped
4 anchovy fillets
2 tablespoons Italian seasoning
2 large onions, sliced into rings
3 cups beef broth

# Readington River Buffalo Company

You can see all sorts of things driving around New Jersey, and if you've traveled the state long enough, you might become a bit blasé. However, even if you think nothing of the wide variety of sights this state offers, you'll still stop dead in your tracks the first time you see the herd of bison at the Readington River Buffalo Company in Readington Township.

Out in the fields, right along route 523, beside the red barns, there are bison grazing. Even at first glance, their behavior is different than typical farm animals. Instead of curiously wandering towards visitors the way that cows or sheep do, the females surround their calves in a protective circle while bulls keep a careful watch from a distance. Approaching a pen of bulls is even more startling. The animals begin a wild but oddly controlled stampede, running from one end of the pen to the other, kicking up huge trails of mud. It is very unusual behavior for captive animals and absolutely engrossing.

The Readington River Buffalo Company is on 235 acres of prime real estate in Hunterdon County with rolling hills, winding lanes, red barns, beautiful homes, and yes—that herd of bison. This all under the watchful eyes of Erick Doyle and his father Gerry. They're located right outside of Flemington, about halfway between New York City and Philadelphia. Even while Gerry worked as a chemist, his family had always kept a few holsteins for beef, but the idea for a bison farm came when the family visited Colorado and saw several operations there. Those places met all the criteria for success: they sold retail, they had a fair amount of freedom over pricing, and there was little competition.

This novelty has worked both for and against them. On one hand, it attracts curious neighbors and many of them become customers, but bison are so unique in New Jersey that they aren't even considered livestock. Instead, they're classified as "exotic animals" and have to be inspected by a separate government agency. Erick speculates that when the farm opened, the state probably had to train somebody for the task.

"Buffalo" is a misnomer. They are correctly called "American bison." This confusion is exacerbated by the popularity of "buffalo mozzarella," a cheese made from a beast only tenuously related to buffalo. But the explanation is simple enough: When the first explorers came to the American prairie, they saw big, brown, shaggy animals in herds and they called them "buffalo" because that was the old world creature they most resembled.

Bison are different from cows in many ways. They pretty much stay off on their own and need very little management. When it's time to move them, they can be lured with food and led through gates from pen to pasture, but most of the time, they make it clear that they'll mind their own business if you mind yours.

Back in the days of the old west, tongue was the most treasured part of the bison, but today this preference is long forgotten. Instead, most customers prefer bison roasts, steaks, and burgers. Erick, a serious cook, is even more ambitious. Slow-braised chuck roasts, bison satays, and Korean specialties like *bul go gi*, the classic barbecue dish or *kal bi* (page 88), a traditional short rib dish, are among his favorites. Of course, this presents a few problems, not the least of which is getting the butcher to cut buffalo ribs short enough to even be called "short."

Gerry and Erick work hard to market their products. Setting up at farmer's markets, something that's often a resounding success for vegetable farmers, doesn't work so well with meat. While the produce stands can offer dazzling displays and beautiful colors, meats must be kept cool, so the entire display consists of a clean table, a couple of coolers, and a list of high prices. Instead, they must try other tactics. Besides local shops, restaurants, and an on-site retail store, they offer bison burgers at fairs and festivals. Not only is this fun and profitable, it gets people interested in what they're doing and brings them back as customers.

"Bison have a whole dynamic that's not like other farm animals," Erick says. "These are basically wild animals surrounded by a fence and that's just something you have to accept. They're territorial, they're dangerous, and they're bigger than you. The herd takes care of itself." Before they had bison, they wondered about these things, but it didn't deter them. "We got them, and we learned."

# Korean-Style Braised Short Ribs (*Kal Bi*)

2 SERVINGS

This dish is a favorite of the guys at the Readington River Buffalo Company but you don't have to use bison ribs. In fact, whether you use beef, pork, lamb, or bison, *kal bi* is a great introduction to Asian-style slow cooking.

Trim the short ribs of any obvious fat. Preheat the oven to 325°F. Combine the onion, garlic, soy sauce, sugar, sesame seeds, ginger, pepper, and oil in a large Dutch oven or soup pot and bring to a boil on top of the stove. Add the ribs, return the mixture to a boil, and then reduce the heat to a simmer. Put the whole thing in the oven and cook for 2 hours, until the meat falls off the bones (bison will take a bit longer). Remove from the oven and let the meat rest at room temperature for 10 minutes before serving.

3 pounds bison or beef short ribs
1 small onion, chopped
6 cloves garlic, chopped or smashed
¼ cup soy sauce
2 tablespoons packed brown sugar
2 tablespoons sesame seeds
2 tablespoons chopped fresh ginger
½ teaspoon ground white pepper
½ teaspoon chile pepper oil

# Bison and Black Bean Chili

4 SERVINGS

In places like Texas and New Mexico, the rules for chili preparation are extremely rigid, with only certain meats, thickeners, and seasonings allowed. Not so in New Jersey, where the state's chili festivals offer stews with chile peppers and every other sort of ingredient as well. This recipe is a conglomeration of the different offerings at a recent festival and gives a sense of the style and variety you can find.

Put the onion, garlic, chipotle, oil, oregano, and cumin in a medium-size pot over medium heat and cook, stirring until the onions are translucent. Add the meat, salt, and pepper and cook until the meat is nicely browned. Lower the heat to a simmer and stir in the peppers, black beans, and corn. Let the whole thing simmer for about 45 minutes, until the meat is completely cooked and the flavors are combined. Serve with rice, tortillas, or cornbread.

1 medium-size onion, chopped (about 1 cup)
8 cloves garlic, chopped
3 or more canned chipotle peppers, chopped
1 tablespoon vegetable oil
1 tablespoon dried oregano
1 teaspoon ground cumin
1 pound shaved (thinly sliced) bison meat, coarsely chopped
1 teaspoon salt
1 teaspoon freshly ground black pepper
2 bell peppers, cut into strips
1 (15½-ounce) can black beans, including the liquid
1 cup fresh or frozen corn

# Southwestern-Style Bison Pasta Sauce

8 SERVINGS

The rich flavor of bison meat makes a perfect base for these southwestern flavors. Freeze half for a future meal. This sauce can be served over all sorts of pasta, especially big, chewy shapes like ziti, conchiglioni, or rigatoni. It's also great over polenta (page 12).

Put the onion, chipotles, garlic, oil, salt, pepper, and cumin in a large skillet over medium heat. Stir occasionally, until the onions are translucent. Add the meat and cook, stirring until it is browned. Add the corn, peppers, and tomatoes. Bring the mixture back to a simmer and let it cook for about 30 minutes, stirring every few minutes to make sure you don't burn the bottom. The sauce is ready when the meat is cooked through.

1 medium-size onion, chopped (about 1 cup)
3 canned chipotle peppers, chopped
4 cloves garlic, chopped
1 tablespoon olive oil
1 teaspoon salt
1 teaspoon freshly ground black pepper
½ teaspoon ground cumin
1 pound ground bison or pork
½ cup fresh or frozen corn
1 bell pepper, cut in strips
1 (15½-ounce) can crushed tomatoes

# Boiled Tongue

4 SERVINGS

Not so long ago, beef tongue was a classic dish and buffalo tongue was considered one of the greatest delicacies. Today, these dishes are all but forgotten and tongue is often discussed in the same breath as organ meats and other "offal." But tongue sandwiches are still on the menu at many Jewish delis and tongue and green sauce (see *chimichurri*, page 126) is a popular dish on Italian and South American tables. If you're able to get a tongue from a good butcher, this recipe is well worth a try. Tongue can be served hot like a roast, or cold as an appetizer or sandwich meat.

Put all of the ingredients in a large pot, cover with water, and bring to a boil. Lower the heat and simmer, covered, for about 1 hour per pound. When the tongue can be easily pierced with a fork, remove it from the pot, put it on a cutting board, and peel off the skin. It should come off easily. Then return the meat to the pot and cook for a few more minutes, or until the flavors of the cooking liquid have penetrated the meat.

**N O T E :** Those of you with great shopping skills or just plain luck may be able to find bison tongue, which is larger than beef, lamb, or veal tongues. The recipe remains the same for all types. Only the quantity of water need vary. Lamb tongues don't need to be peeled.

1 (2½- to 3-pound) beef tongue
1 large onion, quartered
1 carrot, peeled and quartered lengthwise
2 heads garlic, unpeeled, but cut in half widthwise
6 whole black peppercorns
2 bay leaves
1 tablespoon salt

# Stewed Tripe with Chickpeas

4 SERVINGS

Tripe is one of those things that divides meat lovers. You either love it or hate it. There is no dish that can convince a tripe hater to change their ways, but there are dishes that tripe lovers relish. This is a classic dish from Spain that you occasionally find as a special in Newark area restaurants.

Put the chorizo, garlic, oil, oregano, salt, and pepper in a Dutch oven or soup pot over medium heat and cook, stirring until the sausage starts to brown. Stir in the pork. When the sausage, pork, and garlic are well browned, add the onion and stir until any bits of meat that stuck to the bottom of the pan are loosened and the onions are translucent. Add the tripe, peppers, tomatoes, and chickpeas and bring the whole thing to a boil. Reduce the heat to low and simmer for 90 minutes, stirring occasionally, until the pork and tripe are tender. Serve with rice or potatoes as part of a Spanish or Mediterranean meal.

\* There are several types of tripe available. One of the most popular is "honeycomb," which requires 3- 5 hours of simmering before it can be added to this dish. Other types, such as omasum or "bible" tripe, can be cut up and added directly to the dish. Each tripe lover has their own preference. Never argue with them.

**2 small chorizo sausages, diced**

**6 cloves garlic, chopped**

**1 tablespoon olive oil**

**1 tablespoon dried oregano**

**1 teaspoon salt**

**½ teaspoon freshly ground black pepper**

**8 ounces pork loin, cut into 1-inch cubes**

**1 medium-size onion, chopped (about 1 cup)**

**1 pound tripe, cut into 1-inch pieces\***

**1 red bell pepper, cut into strips**

**1 (15½-ounce) can crushed tomatoes**

**1 (15½-ounce) can chickpeas, with the liquid**

# VEGETABLES

# VEGETABLES

Think of a farmer's market and vegetables are what come to mind. Yes, New Jersey produces fruit, meat, and even fish, but vegetables are the heart and soul of its output. Tomatoes are the most visible—red, yellow, or green. They're as small as grapes or as big as grapefruit. During harvest time, they're front and center on every stand! But the range of other items is huge, starting with the first bunch of pencil-thin asparagus in the spring and ending with the last head of cabbage as winter sets in.

There is no real way to keep track of all the vegetables grown in New Jersey. Farmers are always trying something new and different. One week you'll see red, white, or day-glo purple heirloom eggplants. Another time you'll visit a farm stand that has a Chinese green that has never been grown in the U.S. before. Because of this range, there are twice the number of vegetable recipes here than for any other chapter. The displays in our farmer's markets are dominated by vegetables and they are what you're most likely to be attracted to when you stop by the side of the road.

# Olive Oil-Anchovy Dip (Bagna Cauda)

YIELDS 1½ CUPS; 4 SERVINGS

This dish is a northern Italian classic. Serve it as a sauce over roasted or raw peppers, carrots or other vegetables. Although I wouldn't suggest it to an actual Italian food fanatic, It's also great over roasted or baked (or even microwaved) potatoes and mushrooms. This makes a great sauce for steamed shrimp too.

Gently heat 1 tablespoon of the oil in a small saucepan. Add the anchovies and stir until they disintegrate. Next, put in the garlic and sauté until translucent (keep a careful eye on the pan; both the garlic and anchovies burn easily!). Finally, add the salt and remaining oil and simmer over VERY low heat for 20 to 30 minutes.

- 1½ cups olive oil
- 10 anchovy fillets
- 10 cloves garlic, chopped
- 1 teaspoon salt

# Asbury's Natural Village Farm

Asbury, WARREN COUNTY

A sbury's Natural Village Farm sits at a crossroads. With a big red barn and grazing horses, it's visible from all directions. Located at the northwestern edge of Warren County, roughly between the towns of Washington and Clinton, not far from the Delaware River, the farm is nestled in wooded rolling hills where the Musconetcong River carves a deep valley. It's at another sort of crossroads too—a place where the future and the past meet and a passionate farmer combines traditional techniques with the latest in organic cultivation.

Charles Napravnik is the man behind Natural Village Farm. He's a New Jersey native with a lifelong interest in traditional farming. As a young man living in suburban Iselin, he had no firsthand experience, but a strong desire to till the soil. He never considered more practical possibilities like agricultural college. Instead, he hitchhiked down to Lancaster County, Pennsylvania and began a twenty-five-year Amish immersion. "It was just something I wanted to do, go back to the land," he says.

Although he never embraced the Amish faith, he learn the full scope of their non-motorized agricultural techniques, including the skills that serve him today. He also nurtured a deep respect for horses. All his farming is done with draft animals: horses and mules. At first he simply says, "I like driving." (It should be noted here that he uses the word "driving" in its original meaning and is most definitely not talking about cars or trucks!) But Charles goes on to say that, "it brings you a little closer to the land." He also shoes horses all through west-central New Jersey, another skill from his days with the Amish.

Being "closer to the land" is what Asbury's Natural Village Farm is all about. Certified organic and fertilized with the manure from its own horses, the soil is important here. But it's also an outpost of Community Supported Agriculture (CSA). What is this? CSAs are cooperatives of a sort, in which farmers sell shares of the output to member consumers. Here, that means those who own shares help with the harvest, packing, and distribution—an excellent way for food buyers to gain farm experience. What do members get in return? These days there are mostly vegetables with a few berries thrown in, but they are working on bringing chickens and eggs into the mix too. There are always the classics: tomatoes, peppers, and all sorts of greens.

On a freezing day in the dead of winter, the barn still has chile peppers drying and trays of garlic that look ready for peeling and cooking.

When asked about his favorite foods, Charles doesn't hesitate: He immediately starts talking about salad. In the Natural Village Farm kitchen, the most important appliance is the salad spinner. He often dines on nothing but a huge bowl of his farm's produce. Tomatoes and peppers of course, but also kale and chard and anything else that's in season. With a hard-cooked egg or two from one of the farm's free-range chickens, he's got a serious meal.

So what does Charles see in the farm's future? His first answer is grain. "I'd like to grow grain and do a horse harvest." This is an ambitious thought. Grain is almost never grown by non-mechanized farms anymore and this would require the resurrection of a McCormick Harvester, a machine that most of us have only read about in history books. The possibilities offered by heirloom varieties of organic grains must make the heads of artisanal bread makers spin.

Retail markets are also on the way. The farm has an excellent location not far from I-78 (day-trippers can also stop at the Musky Trout Hatchery (see page 36), only a mile or two away) and Charles has been asked to participate in the nearby retail farmer's market in Easton, PA, one of the oldest in the United States. The biggest problem is time. This is essentially a one-man operation and Charles winds up doing everything that needs to be done and then some. Of course, he needs a bit of time to shoe horses too.

# Vegetarian Borscht

4 SERVINGS

There seem to be two versions of borscht, the classic beet soup: a cold, vegetarian one and a hot one with meat. Why not a hot meatless soup? In this recipe, mushrooms are substituted for the beef, pork, or sausage that one normally finds.

Melt the butter in a soup pot over low heat and add the onion, beets, carrots, and garlic. Cook, stirring until the onions are translucent and the garlic starts to brown. Add the mushrooms, cabbage, and salt and pepper to taste, and stir until the cabbage wilts. Now add the broth, turn up the heat, and bring the mixture to a boil. Let it boil for 1 minute, reduce the heat to a simmer, and cover. Cook for 30 more minutes, stirring occasionally, until the beets are tender. Check it to see if it needs more salt and pepper. Serve with sour cream and good dark bread.

\* You can use olive oil and omit the sour cream to make the soup vegan if you wish.

1 tablespoon butter*
1 medium onion, chopped (about 1 cup)
4 ounces beets, scrubbed and chopped (about 1 cup)
1 large carrot, peeled and grated (about ½ cup)
2 cloves garlic, minced
4 ounces mushrooms, chopped (about 1 cup)
1 cup shredded cabbage
Salt
Freshly ground black pepper
3 cups vegetable broth
Sour cream for serving

# Black Bean Soup
# with Beets

6 SERVINGS

Sometimes soup makes all the difference. A container stashed in the freezer can make life much easier on a busy day. And a pot simmering on the stove can make working at home much cozier. This recipe has no meat products, making it a great base for a vegetarian meal. It shouldn't just be reserved for vegetarians though. It's also a fine first course before a roast on a cold night.

Heat the oil in a soup pot over medium heat. Add the oil, sofrito, seasoning, and garlic. Cook, stirring until the garlic starts to become translucent. Add the beets, onion, and peppers and continue stirring. When the onions are translucent, add the beans, broth, spinach, vinegar, salt, and pepper. Simmer for about 45 minutes, stirring occasionally, until the beets are tender.

3 tablespoons olive oil
2 tablespoons *sofrito*
1 tablespoon Italian seasoning
3 garlic cloves, smashed
1 bunch (about 8 ounces) beets, unpeeled, but well-scrubbed and diced
1 medium onion, coarsely chopped (about 1 cup)
1 bell pepper, cut into strips
1 (15½-ounce) can black beans, including the liquid
2 cups vegetable broth
1 (10-ounce) package frozen chopped spinach or 1½ cups cooked spinach
1 tablespoon red wine vinegar
1 teaspoon salt
1 teaspoon freshly ground black pepper

# Curried Beets and Carrots (*Chukandara* and *Gajara Jalfrezi*)

4 SERVINGS

This carrot and beet curry is one of those dishes that somehow never makes it onto typical U.S. Indian restaurant menus, but is quite popular in New Jersey's Indian communities. Serve it as part of an Indian meal with rice and Indian pickles.

Microwave the beets and carrots on high for 4 minutes, until just tender. (They can also be spread on a greased baking sheet and baked at 425°F for 20 minutes.) Then, heat the oil in a large skillet over medium heat and add the curry paste. Mix well. Add the onions and cook, stirring over low heat until tender. Add the carrots and beets and stir until coated. Add ½ cup water and bring to a boil, then reduce the heat and simmer for 15 minutes, until the beets and carrots are tender and have absorbed the curry flavor.

1 bunch (about 8 ounces) beets, unpeeled, but well-scrubbed and diced
2 medium carrots, peeled and diced (about 1 cup)
2 tablespoons vegetable oil
2 tablespoons garam masala curry paste*
1 large onion, diced

* Garam masala curry paste (sometimes just called garam masala paste) is available in most New Jersey supermarkets but can be found at a much lower price in Indian groceries. Do not confuse it with ground garam masala, which is another thing entirely (see Glossary, page 197).

# Springhill
# Farm

Grab a chair and sit down at the edge of a field. Close your eyes and open your other senses. Listen to the sounds of Springhill Farm: helicopters buzzing overhead and jets zooming even higher. Freight trains roaring by with their horns singing the blues … cars, trucks, jackhammers, and a stereo blasting hip-hop or new-wave rock—it's anything but a typical rural experience.

Springhill Farm is notable for many different reasons. Not many farms are walking distance from a jazz club and several fine-dining restaurants. It's also home to the most beautiful farmhouse I've ever seen (it is owned by the Johnson family of first aid fame; none of the crew lives there) and the most youthful and hip farm staff I've encountered. This doesn't change the fact that it's filled with friendly dogs to pet and bees ready to sting, but it still has a weirdly urban feel to it.

Don't be fooled—food grows here: basil, beets, arugula, tomatoes, brussels sprouts, and many different lettuces. There are free-range chickens, rows of potatoes, Swiss chard, kohlrabi, escarole, spinach, and scallions. The woman who makes it all happen is the farm's manager, Amy Longo—she's in her late twenties with a high-energy personality and the sort of strength only farmers have. The soil has penetrated every last square millimeter of her hands and formed patterns like Roman mosaics. When you shake hands with her, the farmer's grip is beyond question.

Amy had a fairly typical Italian-American upbringing in the town of Maplewood, New Jersey. Food was important, but not an obsession. When she went away to college, she studied environmental science and photography. When she graduated, she found a job with a large media company located on Union Square in New York City. On her breaks, she began to explore the Union Square Greenmarket—considered by many to be one of the nation's premier farmer's markets.

It was the greenmarket that both opened her eyes to the world of farming and made it easier for her to adapt to Manhattan life. But the appeal of the land had taken hold and the big city existence was losing its luster. After a year and a half of mass media, Amy found herself as an apprentice on a small farm in Lincoln, Massachusetts, not far from Concord.

Her first paying farm job was as an assistant manager near State College, Pennsylvania. But the manager held a full-time job away from the property and Amy was left in charge most of the time. It was just two and a half acres, but had sheep, chickens, and produce too. There was little help, just a few interns from nearby Penn State University. It kept her very busy!

As much as she liked Pennsylvania, New Jersey was her home. She contacted Karen Anderson of the Northeast Organic Farming Association. Karen is known for matching farms with farmers and is a major source of information for those in the industry. She introduced Amy to Springhill Farm, which was just starting up as a source of produce and herbs for Rats, a very high-end restaurant in Hamilton near Trenton.

Springhill Farm soon expanded beyond Rats and other fine restaurants. They participated in a market in Princeton and were regulars at another in the farm's hometown of Hopewell. These venues gave Amy a far different experience than either the remoteness of State College or the urban intensity of Union Square.

Amy is just beginning to call herself a "farmer." She says, "I'm very young in farmer years," speaking of the depth of experience a person needs to really know this arcane and rapidly changing job. Her promotion to manager this year, after three as assistant manager, boosted her confidence, but also serves to remind her that she has a long journey ahead.

Although she's a vegetarian and a lover of good cooking, Amy freely admits that she works so hard on the farm that she doesn't often have time to eat its food. But when she can, her favorite items are roots. "I am an advocate for beets," she exclaims, holding up a bunch. Springhill Farm grows beautiful, white and golden beets, celeriac—that delicious, but ugly root popular in eastern Europe, and many varieties of potatoes. It is truly paradise for root vegetable fans.

Amy says, "People assume when they see four women that we are just selling…that anybody in the market is just a hired hand, but it's the best opportunity to talk to people about your food. We love it! It's the most satisfying part."

# Eastern European-Style Cabbage Soup

4 SERVINGS

Those little white cubes aren't potatoes! The combination of celery root and bacon give this soup a unique flavor.

Add the bacon to a soup pot over medium heat. When it begins to brown, add the onion, carrots, celery root, mushrooms, and garlic. Cook, stirring until the vegetables begin to brown and then mix in the cabbage. When the cabbage softens a bit, add the broth and bring it to a boil for 1 minute. Reduce it to a simmer for 30 minutes, stirring occasionally, until the celery root is tender. Season with salt and pepper and serve immediately.

4 strips bacon, cut in ½-inch
  pieces
1 small onion, chopped
2 carrots, peeled and chopped
  (about 1 cup)
1 medium celery root, peeled
  and chopped (about 1 cup)
4 ounces chopped mushrooms
  (about 1 cup)
4 cloves garlic, chopped
2 cups chopped cabbage
4 cups chicken or beef broth
2 teaspoons salt
1 teaspoon freshly ground black
  pepper

# Stir-Fried Chinese Cabbage with Scallops

4 SERVINGS

Charlie Wong's vegetables are great inspiration for stir-fry fans. This recipe calls for the more traditional vegetable oil instead of olive oil and Thai fish sauce instead of soy sauce. These changes should give you a good idea of what you can do once you get your stir-fry technique down.

Put a wok on your hottest burner and turn the heat up high. Add the oil and give it a minute to really heat up. Carefully add the peppers, carrot, garlic, chile, and fish sauce and stir. When the garlic starts to brown, add the scallops, cook for a couple of minutes, stirring constantly. Add the cabbage in fistfuls. It will shrink rapidly and within a few moments there will be enough room in the pan. It's ready when the cabbage ribs are tender, about 5 minutes after you start adding the cabbage.

2 tablespoons vegetable oil
1 bell pepper, cut into strips
1 carrot, peeled and grated (about ¼ cup)
4 cloves garlic, chopped
1 dried chile pepper, crumbled
2 tablespoons Thai fish sauce
1 pound sea scallops
4 cups Chinese cabbage, cut into strips

# Red Cabbage Salad

4 SERVINGS

When people talk about salads, they're usually talking about greens. But what about a salad with no greens at all? Here's one that combines two red vegetables. It's a bit different, has a great crunch, and the ingredients are easily found year-round.

Combine the cabbage, carrot, oil, vinegar, caraway, salt, and pepper in a bowl and mix well. Let stand in the refrigerator for at least 1 hour before serving in order to tenderize the cabbage and bring the flavors together.

**VARIATION:** Add 1 or 2 cloves of chopped raw garlic to give the dish some extra power. You'll need to let it stand for at least an extra hour for the garlic flavor to permeate the dish.

3 cups chopped red cabbage
3 carrots peeled and grated
  (about 1 cup)
3 tablespoons walnut oil
2 tablespoon red wine vinegar
1 tablespoon caraway seeds
1 teaspoon salt
1 teaspoon ground white pepper

# Hungarian-Style Cabbage and Noodles

4 SERVINGS

This is a classic Hungarian way of using cabbage and a great dish to serve on a winter evening. Try varying it with the red and savoy varieties or with different pasta shapes.

Bring a pot of salted water to a boil. Cook the noodles for 1 minute less than the package indicates. Drain and reserve.

Melt the butter in a large skillet over medium heat and add the cabbage and onion, stirring frequently to make sure nothing burns. When the onions are translucent and the cabbage has wilted, add the poppy seeds, sugar, pepper, and salt. When they are incorporated, stir in the cooked noodles and cook for 2 more minutes to heat through. Serve immediately.

- 4 ounces egg noodles (about ⅓ of a 12-ounce package)
- 1 tablespoon butter
- 3 cups thinly sliced cabbage
- 1 medium onion, sliced thinly (about 1 cup)
- 1 tablespoon poppy seeds
- 2 teaspoons sugar
- 1 teaspoon ground white pepper
- 1 teaspoon salt

# Race
# Farm

Blairstown, WARREN COUNTY

109

Nestled among rolling hills at the very edge of suburbia, Race Farm is marked by a red barn at a bend in a country road. It's the home of Doug Race, his wife Vickie, their four children, and Doug's dad Carl. Three hundred days a year, it's a quiet spot with fields stretching as far as the eye can see, but when the harvest comes, Race Farm is a destination. It's the place to go for pick your own produce (PYO for short), with every parking space taken and cars lining the roadside for a half mile in either direction. It's PYO that put Race Farm on the map.

Thirty years ago, Race was just another New Jersey family farm. They grew corn, tomatoes, apples, and pumpkins, and watched as the market collapsed and their neighbors went out of business. 1972 was a particularly bad year, when wholesalers offered them ninety cents a bushel for apples, a bit less than it cost to pick them. But just as they were about to give up and let their crop rot, Carl stumbled on a then-unique idea: He took an ad in the Newark *Star-Ledger* that told readers that if they came out to the farm and picked the apples themselves, they could have them for $1.99 a bushel. This was a lot more than the Races could get anyplace else, but also far less than the average price of apples in the supermarket.

A few days after that first ad ran, the apple orchards at Race Farm were packed with people. They picked the trees clean and at that moment, the Races saw their future. "Today we're ninety-five percent retail," Doug Race, the farm's third-generation owner says. In the current world of community farmer's markets and gourmet roadside stands, this doesn't seem so unusual, but back then it was revolutionary. Nobody imagined just how many people were happy to get into their cars and head out to pick and buy quality, local farm produce.

Doug tells a similar story when he talks about community farmer's markets. (He calls these "tailgate markets" because many people imagine farmers driving up in their pickups, lowering their tailgates, and selling out of their trucks.) When his dad had an injury that prevented him from putting in a whole day's work in the fields, he sought out things he could do with his limited range of motion. He came up with the Union Square Greenmarket. From the first

VEGETABLES

moment, they saw that New York customers were both tough and educated. They'd come in snowstorms and they'd come in tornadoes, but they were also really demanding. "They'll buy any quality product you have, I don't care what it is," Doug describes. "They're familiar with different varieties, they know what to do with them, and they pay a fair price for your stuff."

When you walk through a market and come across a Race Farms display, there is no way you would think of a tailgate or the back of any truck. Instead, five or six folding tables form a sort of counter, heaped high with the fruit and vegetables of the season. On a typical early fall Sunday at Summit in Union County, there are bins of unshucked ears of corn, baskets of apples, beets, and a half-dozen other items, plus an area devoted to pies and cookies baked by Doug's wife and daughters. Customers are three and four deep, buying everything in sight.

There are really two kinds of days in the life of Race Farm. With no livestock, there's no need to wake up early and milk the cows. Instead, Doug and his crew spend most of their time out in the fields. (Vickie calls this "hanging out with the rutabagas.") On Manhattan market days, they are up at 3:00 AM and on the road by 4:30—in order to be set up when the first customers arrive. Even as they're setting up at 6:00 in the morning, there are customers waiting at Union Square and they don't stop coming until early evening. This means that Doug leaves Manhattan at the height of rush hour and isn't home until after 8:00 PM. Of course, if they leave the truck unloaded all night, that would invite chaos the next day—everything: crates, cartons, sales displays and unsold produce has to be ready for the morning shift - so they empty it and are back in the house at 9:00 PM.

Three generations of Races have owned the farm, starting in the thirties with Doug's grandpa Carl, Sr. who raised poultry. The family moved on to direct deliveries to supermarkets in the sixties and the current retail efforts that began in the fall of '72. The whole family remains involved. Vickie and their daughters are the bakery, Doug's father is still "the Greenmarket guy," and although their son Ryan has gone away to college, he is majoring in agricultural engineering technology at SUNY Cobbleskill. His goal is to return to the farm and grow tomatoes, corn, and other typical New Jersey crops.

With quality products and great marketing, Race Farm continues to prosper. As Doug says, we do "reasonably well because we grow a little bit of everything."

# Limoncello-Glazed Carrots

4 SERVINGS

Here's a simple dish made with *limoncello*, that delicious Italian liqueur that everybody brings back from the Amalfi coast, but nobody ever finishes. This liqueur, made from lemons, gives a wonderful slightly sweet, citrus flavor to the carrots.

In a small skillet, melt the butter and sauté the onion until translucent. Add the carrots and cook over low heat. When the carrots are almost cooked (about 15 minutes, depending on how thick the slices are), add the *limoncello*, honey, salt, and pepper and stir until the carrots are evenly coated. Cook a few more minutes to make sure that the carrots are tender and the liquid has thickened to a syrup.

\* To save time, microwave the carrots on high for a couple of minutes before adding them to the skillet. This cuts the cooking time by about one third.

1 medium onion, chopped (about 1 cup)
2 teaspoons butter
5 carrots, peeled and thinly sliced\*
¼ cup *limoncello* (Italian lemon liqueur)
2 tablespoons honey
½ teaspoon salt
¼ teaspoon ground white pepper

# Marinated Carrot and Beet Salad

4 SERVINGS

The combination of carrots and beets is one that can be found in both eastern European and Indian cuisines. Don't be scared by these ingredients. It's true that they're the basis of millions of awful school lunch salads, but with fresh vegetables and good preparation, the results will be great.

Preheat the oven to 425°F. Place the beets and carrots on a baking sheet coated with nonstick cooking spray. Bake for 25 minutes. They will be done when the beets are tender enough to stick a fork into. Remove and let cool.

When the vegetables have reached room temperature, add the onion, garlic, oil, vinegar, salt, and pepper. Refrigerate for at least 4 hours and preferably overnight. Serve chilled.

**NOTE:** There is plenty of debate over whether carrots and beets should be peeled. Some people prefer to leave the skins on all root vegetables and others are just as insistent about seeing them all peeled. If you're uncomfortable with the skins, peel them. However, if you choose to keep them on, get yourself a good vegetable brush and scrub them clean.

1 bunch beets, cut into bite-size cubes (about 2½ cups)
2 carrots, peeled and sliced (about 1 cup)
⅓ red onion, sliced
4 garlic cloves, peeled and halved
2 tablespoons extra-virgin olive oil
2 tablespoons red wine vinegar
1 teaspoon salt
½ teaspoon freshly ground black pepper

# Italian-Style Sautéed Cauliflower

4 SERVINGS

This recipe for cauliflower is a pretty exact transcription of how a serious Italian home cook would do it. The only real variation is that the cauliflower is microwaved instead of blanched in boiling water. This saves time, a pot, and a burner.

Put the cauliflower in a microwave-safe bowl with ½ cup water. Microwave on high for about 5 minutes, or until softened. Or simmer in 3 quarts water for 5 minutes. Drain and set aside.

Heat the oil with the anchovies in a large skillet over low heat, stirring occasionally until the anchovies start to disintegrate, 1 or 2 minutes. Increase the heat to medium and add the onion. When the onions are translucent, add the parsley and garlic. After a few more minutes, put in the cauliflower. Mix well, the cauliflower should be evenly coated. Add the salt and pepper and cook, stirring over medium heat for another 10 minutes or until the cauliflower is tender and just begins to brown.

1 head cauliflower,
  cut into 1-inch pieces
2 tablespoons olive oil
3 anchovy fillets
1½ teaspoons dried oregano
1 medium white onion, chopped
  (about 1 cup)
½ cup chopped fresh Italian parsley
4 cloves garlic, chopped
1 teaspoon salt
½ teaspoon freshly ground
  black pepper

# E.R. & Son
# Farm

Middlesex County is pretty built up. It's better known for malls than it is for open spaces, but one rural corner remains. And while Middlesex is not pastoral in the sense of Sussex or Salem, there are still a few farms hanging on. This is where you'll find E.R. & Son.

The road that takes you there is a solid mix of farms and subdivisions. Red barns and three-car garages compete for your attention. This is the front line of a war being fought all over—developers vs. farmers. These are the last stragglers. E.R. & Son, one of the first organic growers in the state, is waging that battle.

Ed Lidzbarski and his wife Rosalie started E.R. & Son back in 1976. He was a printer at the *Home News* and was interested in gardening. He began by growing on the acre surrounding his house and soon started leasing additional fields. As he expanded, so did public awareness of organic foods. At first, only a few macrobiotics would buy from him, but as interest in both local and natural ingredients grew, so did his audience.

Today, Ed's products are found in at least fifteen local health food stores, the Whole Foods Market chain, several farmer's markets, and at the wonderful little store his wife runs right on the farm. Ed grows at least fifty different types of vegetables and one fruit (watermelon). There are white, purple, and brown eggplants; red and yellow grape tomatoes; all sorts of greens, including Malabar spinach (an authentic Indian variety rarely grown here); San Miguel broccoli (tall and thin with an edible stem); beets; and Shunkyo radishes (a cross between daikon and traditional varieties).

Organic farmers both love and need variety in their fields. Ed says that, "In my perfect world, I would be growing more things and less of everything." This diversity would enrich the soil and act as a natural buffer against disease. He is always ready to try the new and open to suggestions from customers and retailers. In February and March, he sits down with buyers and plans the year's crops with them.

Because E.R. has such demanding clientele, the pace here gets pretty hectic during harvest time. Ed begins his day by picking up his workers in nearby Freehold and spends most of it harvesting, packing, bunching, and sorting. He is famous for mixed pints of red and yellow grape tomatoes. These have to be chosen by hand and carefully checked before they go out to markets and stores.

"People buy with their eyes," complains Ed as he talks about all this work. He points out that a tomato with a few blemishes would taste exactly the same as a flawless one and laments that the need to provide perfect produce causes him great anguish and expense. "The pesticides we organic farmers can use cost a fortune! And if people would take a few spots, we wouldn't need them at all," he points out. But he knows how demanding the market is and does his best to stay on top of it.

Like many farmers profiled here, Ed doesn't own the land he farms on. The farm store is always in Monroe Township on Route 522, but this year, he is farming a different set of fields down the road in Colt's Neck. This notion is one that's hard to accept. Most of us see a farm when we whiz by in our car and imagine that it's been in the same family for generations, but in fact, most New Jersey farmland is in the hands of developers who are either waiting for the right moment to build or hoping for a change in zoning regulations. In the meantime, people like Ed farm their land, sometimes for a year or two, sometimes for decades. Each growing season, there's a game of musical chairs as the demand for local foods goes up and the amount of acreage available to produce it goes down.

The scramble is on. Like most farmers in this part of the state, Ed and Rosalie are torn between their love of working the land and the challenge of doing so within a short drive of one of the nation's largest cities. "There's nothing I'd like more than to have a simple lifestyle where I don't have to make tons of money," Ed wishes, but then he starts talking about the proximity to his customers and the joy they show when they find a place like this so close by. It doesn't look like he's fleeing anytime soon.

E.R. + SON FARM

ORGANIC PRODUCE

115

VEGETABLES

# Roasted Celery Root

4 SERVINGS

Is celery root the ugliest vegetable in the market? Maybe, but once it's peeled, seasoned, and roasted, it's a whole different thing entirely. You might also find it sold under the name celeriac.

Preheat the oven to 400°F. With a small amount of the oil, lightly grease a baking sheet.

Sprinkle the celery root cubes with the seasoning, salt, and pepper and then spread them out along with the garlic on the baking sheet. Drizzle with the remaining olive oil. Bake them for about 45 minutes, or until golden brown and tender enough to easily pierce with a toothpick.

¼ cup olive oil
3 cups peeled and cubed celery root (1 large root, about 16 ounces)
1 tablespoon Italian seasoning
Salt
Freshly ground black pepper
4 cloves garlic, coarsely chopped

# Japanese Flavor Cucumber Salad

4 SERVINGS

Cucumbers are an unsung hero of the farm stand. With a long growing season and good storage qualities, they're available for a long time. And compared to the strange, waxed things you see all too often in the supermarket, they have an appealing look. However, using them can be a challenge, pickles are common enough and they do work in salads, but why not a bowlful of them on their own?

Put the cucumbers in a bowl and toss with the vinegar, oil, and salt. Sprinkle with the seasoning. Serve chilled.

* What is furikake? It's the crunchy stuff that sushi chefs sprinkle on certain rolls. You also find Japanese food enthusiasts dusting it over everything: salads, soba, and cooked rice dishes. You can find it in all the big Asian stores, but I warn you—when you buy it, you'll sprinkle it on everything you eat for the first couple of days; it's addictive!

3 cucumbers, thinly sliced (about 3 cups; a mandoline is perfect for this)
2 tablespoons rice vinegar
1 tablespoon sesame oil
1 teaspoon salt
1 tablespoon Japanese mixed seasoning (*furikake*)* or toasted sesame seeds

# The Philly Chile Company

With a name like The Philly Chile Company, you might think this is a southwestern-style restaurant in downtown Philadelphia, not a farm in that city's suburbs. But a farmhouse built in the 1740s and a lone tethered goat watching over seven acres of organic fields, make the Philly Chile Company most definitely a New Jersey Farm.

The company was founded by New Jersey native Amanda McCutcheon and her husband, Rob Ferber, almost a decade ago. Amanda had years of experience as a professional cook and had worked at a restaurant in Brunswick, Maine, that had its own organic farm. But she had family in New Jersey, an MFA from Columbia, and relatives with a farm in Chester County, Pennsylvania, she felt that Maine was just "too out of the loop" and moved to Philadelphia. After working in town for a while, the couple bought a property in nearby Salem County, New Jersey.

Here, the land is flat for as far as the eye can see. Farms aren't nestled into valleys or perched on scenic hilltops. Instead, the land is cultivated for miles on end and the only natural breaks are rivers that sometimes look more like swamps. Somehow this area missed all the booms that New Jersey has spawned.

Originally, the idea was to bring back chile varieties from New Mexico and raise them here. They quickly discovered, however, that it wasn't going to work. The chiles grew well in the south Jersey soil, but they were unable to dry them correctly in the humid climate. This problem didn't stop them from keeping their great name, however, or from growing them fresh.

Chiles weren't the only setback. One morning, they woke up to find their flock of free-range chickens stolen. They took this as a sign that they should return to the New Jersey farming classics: heirloom tomatoes, Italian and Asian eggplant varieties, cabbages, and all sorts of root vegetables. Overwhelmingly though, the most popular crop is garlic. Customers call it "juicy," almost as if it were a meat, a clear reaction to the typical dried commercial product.

Since they're certified organic, they must practice traditional crop rotation to keep their soil at its best, and because of this, they must vary the produce they offer year by year. These include those chiles, blackberries, raspberries, strawberries, a whole bunch of cabbage varieties, tomatoes, onions, and of course, that great garlic.

Rob, Amanda's husband, doesn't work on this farm, but he is in the field and serves as a member of the Salem County Board of Agriculture. Rob and Amanda see the board as an example of the growing role of organics in Salem. Just five or six years ago, organic farmers were viewed as part of the lunatic fringe, but these days, their success is well known.

Adrift in an ocean of farm strands, the Philly Chile Company doesn't have one of its own. Instead, they rely on word of mouth, a Web page, and a presence at two local markets: Salem and Bridgeton. Both give Amanda the chance to "talk organic" with locals, many of whom farm themselves.

Having cooked professionally, Amanda is a serious cook and food-lover. Her favorite restaurants include Philadelphia fine-dining hot spots like Alma de Cuba and Morimoto. Asked her favorite cuisine, she immediately names "Asian." Amanda frequently cooks classic noodle dishes like pad thai. As a graduate student at Columbia, she had a roommate who had lived in Korea and taught her how to prepare kimchee. While she doesn't have vats of the stuff fermenting in the yard, she does frequently cook Korean dishes.

Down in this part of New Jersey, survival is in itself success. As she talks, she describes her vision of the future—a southern New Jersey where local, organically raised food is what people eat every day and consumers happily buy from their local farmers.

# Middle Eastern–Style Cold Eggplant (Baba Ghanouj)

6 SERVINGS

This classic dish is found all over the Middle East and uses one of New Jersey's most important vegetable crops—the eggplant. It's served as a topping, sandwich filling or among a plate of appetizers as a dip.

Preheat the oven to 400°F. Spread the eggplant on a non-stick baking sheet and season with salt and pepper. Bake for 40 minutes, until tender, and allow to cool.

Toss the eggplant, garlic, lemon juice, oil, salt, and pepper together in a large bowl until well combined. Then pass through a food mill. (A food processor will work too, but it doesn't offer the same texture.) Sprinkle the top with the sumac. Put the baba ghanouj in the refrigerator for at least 4 hours before serving.

2 large eggplants, peeled and cut into 1-inch cubes
2 teaspoons salt, plus extra as needed
1 teaspoon freshly ground black pepper
4 garlic cloves, coarsely chopped
1 tablespoon lemon juice
2 tablespoons olive oil
½ teaspoon ground sumac

# Grilled Eggplant in Thai Green Curry Sauce

2 SERVINGS

Unlike many curries in which the principal ingredient and the spices are cooked in the same pot, in this dish grilled eggplant is served with a separately made spicy sauce. This sauce is nothing more than curried onions and can easily be made in advance and even frozen if need be.

Separate the coconut milk: Take a can that's been sitting on the shelf for at least a full day and open it without shaking it. You'll see a thick cream at the top. Carefully spoon out the cream without mixing in the thinner milk at the bottom.

Next, heat the oil in a skillet over low heat. Add the coconut cream and stir until melted (This will look very much like melting butter.). Add the tamarind and curry pastes and mix thoroughly. Add the onion and cook, stirring until a liquid forms. Add the mango juice, remaining coconut milk, and 3 cups water and simmer over low heat until the onion disintegrates and the sauce is the consistency of a thick syrup—about 2 hours. You can speed things up by puréeing the sauce after as little as 45 minutes of cooking, but you must reduce the amount of water to 1½ cups. However, the long cooking breaks down the onion and deepens the flavor.

**GREEN CURRY SAUCE**
1 (13½-ounce) can coconut milk
1 tablespoon vegetable oil
1 tablespoon tamarind paste
3 tablespoons Thai green curry paste
1 large onion, chopped (about 1½ cups)
⅓ cup mango juice
1 large Italian eggplant, cut into ½-inch-thick slices
½ cup olive oil
1 tablespoon salt
1 tablespoon freshly ground black pepper

Meanwhile, **START ON THE EGGPLANT:** Preheat a grill to medium heat and oil the rack. Brush the eggplant with the olive oil and season them with salt and pepper. Grill until cooked through, turning once, about 6 minutes. The eggplant can also be cooked in a grill pan on the stove. Pour the sauce over the eggplant slices and serve.

# Curried Thai Eggplant

2 SERVINGS

Thai curries aren't really that different from Indian ones when it comes to technique. First you mix a base of oil and a paste of spices (the ingredients in a commercial curry paste), and then the vegetable or meat is added and cooked in the mixture. However, be aware that as with all the other recipes that call for it, coconut milk requires a bit of careful handling. Read the instructions carefully before you open the can.

**1 (13½-ounce) can coconut milk**
**2 tablespoons Thai red curry paste**
**6 to 8 Thai eggplants (about 12 ounces), stemmed and quartered***
**1 medium onion, chopped (about 1 cup)**
**¼ cup orange juice**
**6 fresh Thai basil leaves, torn into small pieces (use Italian basil if Thai is not available)**

Separate the coconut milk: Take a can that's been sitting for a good long while and gently place on the counter. Open it without shaking it. You should see a thick cream at the top. Carefully spoon out the cream without mixing in the thinner milk at the bottom.

Add the cream and curry paste to a medium skillet and stir over low heat until they're blended. Add the eggplant and onion. Cook, stirring over low heat—this dish burns easily—until the onion and eggplant are tender and fully cooked, about 30 minutes. Add the basil and mix thoroughly. Serve hot with rice as part of an Asian meal.

* If you can't find Thai eggplant, use the long, thin, purple ones and cut them into 1-inch pieces.

# Cold Sicilian-Style Eggplant

8 SERVINGS

Sicilian cuisine is filled with methods of preserving vegetables in ways that modern technology just can't catch up with. This dish can be kept in the refrigerator for at least a week and canners can go to town. Serve this with Italian bread, olives, and other antipasto items. Most people spoil this dish by serving it in the vinegar it's preserved in. Try draining the eggplant and drizzle it with olive oil, salt and pepper. This mellows the flavor quite a bit.

Combine the vinegar, garlic, chiles, and salt in a large pot with 3 cups water and bring to a boil. Reduce the heat and cook for 10 minutes. Add the eggplant and simmer for 10 more minutes, until the eggplant is tender. Stir frequently to make sure all the eggplant is covered with liquid. Put the cooked eggplant in a container and add enough cooking liquid to cover. Cool for several hours before serving.

- 2 cups white wine vinegar
- 2 heads of garlic, unpeeled, but halved
- 4 dried chile peppers
- 1 tablespoon sea salt
- 2 large eggplants, cut into ¼-inch strips*

* Opinions vary on the best size for the eggplant strips. Sometimes they're cut as fine as matchsticks, and sometimes even thicker than this recipe calls for. Think of the strips like French fries and vary the thickness to your own taste.

# Well-Sweep Herb Farm

Port Murray, WARREN COUNTY

Visit Well-Sweep on a warm Indian summer day. It's the sort of scene you hope for when you head for the country. The farmhouse, painted powder blue, was built in 1820. There are flowers blooming, the red barn gift shop is bathed in warm morning light, and the roosters are crowing like there is no tomorrow.

It's easy to get carried away at Well-Sweep. The landscaping is perfect and the animals are friendly. Walk up to the rabbit cages and you expect them to start talking like characters in a Disney film, but it's all very real—the result of great effort by Cyrus Hyde and his wife Louise.

When they bought the place in 1967, it was a wreck. The fields were overgrown, and all there was were a few sheep. But Cyrus and Louise had a plan, organic farming, food self-sufficiency, and a better life for their young children. However, Cyrus wasn't the sort of person who'd be comfortable with only a plot of land and some jars of food on the shelves. He has the mind and spirit of a collector, and pretty soon, his collection started to grow.

Back in '67, Cyrus and Louise were living in Totawa on the remaining acre of what had once been the Hyde family farm. Cyrus had always lived with horses and livestock and was working as a landscaper, but he wanted a real homestead. His first thought was dairy, but he soon made a surprising discovery: He was allergic to dairy cows! Herbs seemed like a reasonable second choice. They required everything that Cyrus and Louise brought to the table: intelligence, creativity, and that collector's instinct. There was another factor too—Cyrus had herbs in his family.

As far back as the American Revolution, his ancestors were picking and selling medicinal herbs. His great-great-great-great-grandmother, Clara Van Houten, served as an herbal medicine practitioner with George Washington's troops. This knowledge was handed down through the family. Cyrus talks about how during his childhood, herbs were hung to dry in the wagon house. His mother took him there and taught him about the different plants. "This was gathered in the mountains…" or "This came from the meadow," were the typical beginnings of her herbal lessons.

By the time Louise found a bit of property for them to farm, the plan was in place. Well-Sweep began with four and a half acres and was soon producing herbs and feeding the growing Hyde family. It didn't stay that size for long. They purchased more land and grew over twenty-fold. Soon afterwards, the herb business became one of the world's largest, with over 1,800 varieties.

"We had a way of life, raised our food organically. We built the land organically," Cyrus reflects. Soon Rodale Press, the publisher of natural lifestyle books and periodicals, took an interest in Well-Sweep and did several articles and a film on them. Cyrus doesn't see this as the fruit of his efforts though. "The Lord has blessed us with free advertising," is how he explains it.

What grows at Well-Sweep Herb Farm? So much that it's hard to take it all in. Begin with the sage: Longwood Blue, Russian, and Filigram Russian; there are fourteen culinary sages and twenty-five ornamentals. Next there are eleven different kinds of poppies. The turtleheads alone range from White Turtlehead to Hot Lips Turtlehead. Their catalog has seventy-five pages of herbs listed in small print!

Well-Sweep's Elizabethan Knot Garden is a re-creation of the formal herb gardens of 400 years ago. There are also a group of specifically bred show chickens on display as well as the livestock and vegetable patch that feeds the family.

The farm is remarkably self-contained. The Hydes only sell their herbs on site. They have never offered anything wholesale or sold at farmer's markets. Their shop is a complete resource for herb enthusiasts, with books and tools. They also have a large dried flower section.

Do the Hydes consume these herbs themselves? When Cyrus talks about his favorite foods, he rattles off a list of herbal recipes created by his wife. Her cookbook, *Favorite Recipes From Well-Sweep* (Morris Press), available from the farm's shop, is one of the store's best sellers. Restaurant food? If you guessed Thai, one of the most herbaceous cuisines on the planet, you'd be right. He names it without thinking more than a millisecond. He has plenty of good words about Indian food too.

On busy days, Cyrus strolls the grounds and chats with customers. He often hands out samples with surprising flavors and fragrances for visitors. He crushes allspice and bay rum leaves and out come the pungent fragrance of after-shave lotion. Those leaves perfumed my car for days.

# Parsley and Garlic Sauce (*Chimichurri*)

1 PINT; 8 SERVINGS

This sauce was inspired by the Italian version (called *salsa verde*) used on boiled meats and the Argentinean (*chimichurri*) for steaks. It's great with grilled meat from Simply Grazin' (page 76), Readington River Buffalo Company (page 86), or Neptune Farms (page 82). A few dried herbs such as oregano and thyme, from Well-Sweep (page 124) will help too. Roasted chicken or turkey works too, but for an unusual twist, try it with the Kofta Kebabs (page 79).

In a blender or food processor, combine the oil, parsley, vinegar, garlic, and anchovies on high until they form a smooth paste. Add the onion, peppers, and basil and blend until they are finely chopped and well distributed in the liquid. Put the capers in last and just process for a few seconds to mix them in. Pour the sauce into a resealable container and put it in the refrigerator. Give it a stir every hour or so, for the first few hours. It can be served after 4 hours and will keep for several days stored in the refrigerator.

**VARIATION:** Add a pinch or two of fresh thyme, rosemary, or oregano.

1 cup extra-virgin olive oil
1 cup chopped fresh Italian parsley
¼ cup white wine vinegar
6 cloves garlic
4 anchovy fillets
½ small red onion
2 small dried red chile peppers
3 fresh basil leaves
1 tablespoon capers

# Portuguese Kale Soup (*Caldo Verde*)

4 SERVINGS

It has been said that Portugal is one of the great soup countries and that *caldo verde* (green soup) is one of its finest. Most of the ingredients are easily available at New Jersey farm markets and the chorizo can be found in Portuguese or Latino groceries.

Bring 4 cups water to a boil in a soup pot. Add the chorizo, pork, potatoes, carrots, and salt and return the mixture to a boil. Reduce the heat to a simmer and cook, stirring occasionally, for about 30 minutes, or until the pork is tender and the vegetables are softening. Add the kale and beans and cook for another 30 minutes, or until the pork is very tender.

* Almost any type of potato will work, but each will give a slightly different texture. I like Yukon Golds, but don't be afraid either to experiment or just use what you have on hand.

**VARIATIONS:** If your knife skills are up to it, chop the ingredients very finely for a very different soup. For something even more refined, put the finished soup into the food processor and purée for a moment. You can also substitute beef or even pig's feet for the pork and still meet the definition of *caldo verde*.

8 ounces chorizo sausage, cut into bite-size cubes
8 ounces boneless pork loin, cut into 1-inch cubes
8 ounces potatoes, cubed (about 2 cups)*
3 carrots, peeled and sliced (about 1 cup)
1 teaspoon salt
1 bunch kale, chopped (about 3 cups)
1 (15½-ounce) can white beans, including the liquid

# Oak Shade
# Farm

Denville, MORRIS COUNTY

Some New Jersey farms are in deeply remote places and can make you feel like you're at the end of the world. Others are awfully close to suburbia and walking distance from Starbucks shops, doctor's offices, or even jazz clubs. But only one commercial, producing New Jersey farm is actually a suburban house. Here, in the space of a typical back yard, there is enough cultivation going on to fill a market stand on a weekly basis.

What can be grown on a patch that measures about 30 x 50 feet, can earn you a living and not bring the police over? Shiitake mushrooms!

This isn't why Alex Adams, the owner of Oak Shade Farm raises shiitakes, he would grow them no matter where he lived. "Shiitake are the most challenging mushrooms, pound for pound," he says. They require all sorts of effort: a clean place to inoculate the logs, scientific skills to handle the spores, and a precise control of humidity in an outdoor setting.

Lucky for Oak Shade's neighbors, mushroom farming is a very quiet activity. All one sees are attractive piles of oak logs that look a bit like split rail fences. They are the medium upon which the mushrooms grow. Alex drills holes, fills them with the seeds (called "spores"), and stacks the timber in a shady spot. Then, with the right combination of light, temperature, and humidity, the wood will fruit and with astounding speed, they will be flush with shiitake and ready to pick.

With a thin, wiry physique, a gray beard, and a quiet, thoughtful manner, Alex is the sort of man who appears to have been both a farmer and scholar all his life. Mushroom books, magazines, and newsletters are scattered around his house. You're clearly in the hands of an expert. In addition to growing shiitake commercially in his yard, he studied them at Rutgers, belongs to the New Jersey Mycological Association, and forages for wild specialties.

Shiitake fans seem to be divided over whether they should be eaten fresh or dried and Oak Shade Farm offers them both ways. But it's the fresh you're likely to see when you find Alex and his partner Carol at a local farmer's market. There, the experts study the crop for the cracking in the caps that denotes quality. This effect, called danko, shows that the mushrooms were grown outside and experienced a wide variety of temperatures, ensuring a greater depth of flavor. Shiitakes grown on factory farms just look like flat and brown.

Farmer's markets are where you'll find Alex. He can't very well open a stand on his suburban cul-de-sac (although a neighbor or two will buy some every now and then), so he sets up shop at Lafayette in New Jersey and in Hell's Kitchen in Manhattan. There he'll meet his fans face to face. Like most of the farmers who make the trip, he's deeply impressed by the way Manhattanites react to his crop. They're knowledgeable, demanding, and willing to pay a good price for a quality product.

Alex himself eats shiitakes all the time, prepared in every way imaginable, but prefers them dried. He pulls out large glass jars of perfectly preserved mushrooms riddled with beautiful danko patterns and starts talking about the pleasures of shiitake consumption. For him, a serving of shiitakes sautéed in olive oil with garlic and a bit of brown rice on the side is an ideal meal, but he also enjoys them stir-fried with seasonal vegetables. There's more: He eats shiitake soups and slow-cooked stews too. In fact, their fibrous structure is better suited to long cooking methods than any other cultivated mushroom.

Alex works hard on his small shiitake patch, but he feels he could handle more. Actively searching for a larger piece of land, he could easily grow four times as much or perhaps have a market vegetable garden. But wherever he goes, his expertise in producing this very unusual crop will come along with him.

# Marinated Mushrooms

6 SERVINGS

Mushrooms aren't all that common in New Jersey farmer's markets, so when they do show up, there's some excitement in the kitchen.

To cook the mushrooms: Bring 4 quarts salted water to a boil and add the mushrooms. Lower the heat to a simmer, and cook, stirring occasionally, for about 5 minutes. The mushrooms should be completely moist throughout. Drain.

Mix the cooked mushrooms, onion, garlic, parsley, vinegar, oil, salt, and pepper together in a large bowl and toss until they're well combined. Cover and refrigerate for at least 8 hours before serving. The dish will continue to improve for several days.

8 ounces fresh shiitake mushroom caps, cut in bite-size pieces
½ small red onion, chopped
4 cloves garlic, chopped
¼ cup chopped fresh Italian parsley
¼ cup white wine vinegar
2 tablespoons olive oil
1 teaspoon salt
½ teaspoon freshly ground black pepper

# Mushrooms Stuffed with Chicken and Spinach

4 SERVINGS

If you're lucky enough to get your hands on some great mushroom caps – perhaps beautiful shiitake or even just some nice portobellos—this is a change from than the regular egg and bread crumb filling. Don't hesitate to vary the seasonings or even the type of meat. There is no reason to ever stuff a mushroom the same way twice.

Preheat the oven to 325°F. Grease a baking sheet.

Mix the chicken, spinach, egg, oil, seasoning, garlic salt, and pepper together in a large bowl. When they are completely blended, spoon the mixture into the mushroom caps. Place them on the prepared baking sheet, stuffed sides up, and put them in the oven. Bake for 40 minutes, until the filling is cooked and the mushrooms are tender. Serve warm.

1 pound ground chicken
1 cup cooked and drained spinach or 1 (10-ounce) package frozen chopped spinach, thawed
1 egg
2 tablespoons olive oil
1 tablespoon Italian seasoning
2 teaspoons garlic salt
½ teaspoon freshly ground black pepper
8 large mushroom caps

# Mushroom Chili

4 SERVINGS

Chili takes many forms in New Jersey (see Buffalo and Black Bean Chili, page 89). You can find it both with and without beans, but also with beans they don't even know about in other parts of the country. Traditional chili from the Southwest contains only meat and seasonings (no beans). This recipe keeps those seasonings, but uses chopped shiitake mushrooms instead of meat. Alex Adams from Oak Shade Farm (see page 128) would be very pleased.

Heat the oil in a large soup pot. Add the cilantro, chile powder, paprika, oregano, cumin, salt, and pepper over low heat. Add the garlic and cook, stirring until it starts to brown. Add the onion and cook until translucent. Stir in the mushrooms and cook for another 3 or 4 minutes. Add 2 cups water, mix well, and bring the chili to a boil. After 2 minutes, lower the heat to a simmer. Let it cook uncovered, stirring occasionally, until the liquid has evaporated into a thick sauce, about 1 hour.

2 tablespoons vegetable oil
¼ cup chopped fresh cilantro or
   2 tablespoons dried cilantro
2 tablespoons ancho chile
   powder
2 tablespoons Hungarian sweet
   paprika
1 tablespoon dried oregano
1½ teaspoons ground cumin
1 teaspoon salt
1 teaspoon ground white pepper
10 cloves garlic, chopped
   (about ¼ cup)
1 medium onion, chopped
   (about 1 cup)
8 ounces (about 4 cups)
   chopped shiitake mushrooms

# Sautéed Kale and Shiitake Mushrooms

2 SERVINGS

This is a great main dish for vegetarians or a side dish with a piece of meat. Lots of garlic and herbs create flavors that are very strong, but on a cold night when kale and shiitakes are the things that look best in the market, this dish works. Don't be put off by the fact that this recipe uses twelve cups of ingredients. Everything shrinks during cooking.

Heat the oil in a large skillet over a low flame. Add the onion, peppers, garlic, anchovies, and oregano and cook, stirring until the onions are translucent. Add the kale. When the kale is wilted and shrinks a bit, stir in the mushrooms and add the broth. Cook over low heat, stirring occasionally, for about 20 minutes, or until the mushrooms are completely tender.

**N O T E :** This is also a great dish to make with dried Shiitake. You'll need 2 cups of caps broken into bite-size pieces. Place them in a heatproof bowl. Bring 4 cups water to a boil and pour over the mushrooms. Let them soak about 30 minutes, drain and proceed with the recipe.

1 tablespoon olive oil
1 medium onion, chopped
  (about 1 cup)
3 chile peppers, chopped
6 cloves garlic, chopped
3 anchovy fillets
1 teaspoon dried oregano
1 bunch kale, chopped
  (about 6 cups)
8 ounces fresh shiitake
  mushrooms, sliced
  (about 4 cups)
1 cup vegetable broth

# Upper Meadows
# Farm

Len Pollara, the owner of Upper Meadows Farm, warns people "not to expect anything glamorous" when they come visit. While it's hard to imagine anybody expecting glamour from a visit to a farm in one of New Jersey's most rural corners, the fact that it's owned by a successful jazz and salsa trombonist might make guests suspect otherwise.

Upper Meadows Farm is just about at the northern tip of the state. It's only a few moments drive from both New York and Pennsylvania. Getting there means a long trip up a two-lane road followed by a jaunt down a private gravel drive appropriately called "Pollara Lane." The farm begins where the lane ends. Park your car by the pasture, right in front of the free-range chickens. Here you'll find of Upper Meadows' fields and the Pollara family home.

This farm is really out in the country. Unlike many others in the state, there are no views of office buildings or neighboring condo complexes. Instead, each field here is nestled in its own patch of woods and boundaries are as often delineated by centuries-old stone walls as they are by steel wire. "Encroachment" here means bears and coyotes, not corporate warehouses or industrial parks.

The history of Upper Meadows Farm is as rocky as its soil. It's a substantial part of what was once the Pollara Farm, where Len spent part of his childhood as his father and uncle gradually saw their farm diminish. What could once have sustained an extended family was broken up and sold piece by piece. Back in the seventies, when Len was playing trombone full time, he dreamed of buying back a piece of that land to farm. He had the chance to buy four and a half acres in 1986 and had it paid off in four years. Then he added another six, and after that, a few more bits here and there. Today, he owns fifty acres and leases another 103.

Upper Meadows Farm is not just natural—it's certified organic. This means that Len complies with the standards set forth by the USDA and is inspected by NOFA-NJ, a non-profit organization that is accredited to provide this service. Being organic has been a priority for Len since his teen years. Back then he injured himself mishandling some chemicals and spent his recovery time studying the alternatives.

Besides chickens and cows, over seventy varieties of vegetables are grown here. Len beams with pride as he names them: magenta, black seeded Simpson, and red oak leaf lettuce; Jacob's cattle, Vermont cranberry, giant lima, and Roma beans; black, neon, spooky (white) long Japanese eggplants; Asian greens including bok choy, tatsoi, han sai tai, and Chinese cabbage; Russian red kale and curly kale; butte, red lasoda, German butterball, rose finn apple, fingerling, and Viking purple potatoes; hot and sweet, gourmet, red knight, habanero, and cherry bomb peppers; northern pickling cucumbers; chioggia, bull's blood, and early wonder tall top beets; scarlet nantes and chantilly carrots; daikon radishes and purple top turnips. Catching his breath, he realizes that he didn't even mention broccoli or cabbage or grains or….

"This was a successful year for market development," is Len's answer when asked about how he's doing. Like most other growing New Jersey farms, Upper Meadows concentrates on retail, but they go beyond that. They have a CSA program that allows individuals to purchase a share of the harvest, a buying club where people can pick up a fixed amount of produce every week, and an active presence at the markets around Sussex County. They see their biggest crowds at the lively market at Lafayette. They're also at sites they've developed themselves, most notably at the headquarters of Selective Insurance in Branchville—a location with over 800 employees. Of course, they also sell at the farm itself.

Len may travel the world when he's playing the trombone, but when it's time to eat, his mind is always on the farm. Wherever he goes, he evaluates the food. Is it fresh? How close to organic is it? When he talks about food, he never mentions the names of dishes, only the quality of what he's presented. "My favorite is fresh," is how he sums it up.

In the end, you realize what "glamour" means in this case. Len Pollara knows glamour; he's a professional musician with many recordings under his belt. But when it's all said and done, he's back on the farm. Those clearings in the forest high above the Delaware River are the center of his life. He could have done many other things, but he chose to be here, he fought to be here. As he says when he strolls the fields on a late fall day, "The soil is our wealth."

# Sautéed Okra

4 SERVINGS

Okra is one of the stranger looking vegetables. It has none of the leafy appeal of a salad green, none of the elegance of an eggplant, and none of the notoriety of broccoli. No president has ever talked about it and people don't wax nostalgic for it. But we in New Jersey certainly eat it! It grows all over, and is worth a try. Here's the classic southern European method.

Heat the oil in a small skillet over medium-low heat. Add the garlic and cook, stirring until the garlic just begins to brown. Add the okra, salt, and pepper and stir occasionally. During the first few minutes, it will be slimy and look awful, but don't despair—just keep cooking over low heat. After about 30 minutes, the slime will vanish and the okra will be nicely browned and ready to serve.

2 tablespoons olive oil
4 cloves garlic, minced
2 cups ¼-inch-thick okra slices
1 teaspoon salt
½ teaspoon freshly ground
   black pepper

# Onions Stewed in Japanese Vinegar

4 SERVINGS

Onions never seem to be served on their own, although we eat them all the time. However, there are times in the dead of winter when nothing else can be found. And, onions can carry a dish by themselves. Most of the recipes for this dish use wine or cider vinegar, but here, Japanese vinegar gives this dish a nice twist.

Bring the broth to a boil and add the vinegar and salt. Reduce to a simmer and add the onions. Cook until tender, about 15 minutes.

\* Homemade broth is great if you have it. If not, feel free to use the many packaged broths available in supermarkets or one of the interesting bouillon cubes available in Asian markets. An unusual favorite is Knorr's Chinese ham flavor.

2 cups chicken or vegetable broth*
½ cup Japanese rice vinegar
½ teaspoon salt
2 large onions, quartered, or 2 cups small onions

# Onion and White Bean Pasta Sauce

1 QUART; 4 SERVINGS

This sauce has enough depth of flavor to stand up to the new whole wheat organic pastas that are appearing in stores these days. Try it with spaghetti or other long shapes. It also works nicely over fish or vegetables. It's a refreshing change for people who just can't handle another meal of pasta with tomato or pesto sauce.

Heat the oil in a medium skillet over low heat. Mix in the salt, seasoning, and pepper and add the onions and parsley. Stir occasionally for about 45 minutes. At this point, the onions will be quite soft and some liquid will have formed. Add the beans and wine. Simmer, stirring every few moments, until most of the liquid has evaporated and a thick sauce remains, about 15 minutes.

2 tablespoons olive oil
1½ teaspoons salt
1 teaspoon Italian seasoning
¼ teaspoon freshly ground black pepper
3 large yellow onions, sliced into rings
1 cup chopped fresh parsley
1 (15½-ounce) can white beans
1 cup dry white wine.

# Stir-Fried Squid and Onions in Black Bean Sauce

4 SERVINGS

The soft, dark soil of northern New Jersey is famous for its onions. All too often though, they wind up as the background for other ingredients. Here they add sweetness, texture and act as carrier for the black bean sauce. Serve this as part of a Chinese meal with rice.

Heat a wok on your hottest burner. Add the oil and give it a minute to get hot. Then, add the black bean sauce and blend it with the oil. Carefully put in the onion, pepper, and soy sauce and stir. When the onions are limp and translucent, add the squid. Cook for a couple of minutes, stirring constantly. It's ready when the squid is cooked through, about 8 minutes. Serve right away or the squid will toughen up.

**N O T E :** If you use frozen squid (and this is often the best choice) do NOT defrost it in a microwave! They will turn into rubber before your eyes. Just let it thaw in the fridge.

2 tablespoons vegetable oil
1 tablespoon black bean garlic sauce
1 onion, sliced into thin rings
1 red or yellow bell pepper, sliced into thin strips
1 tablespoon soy sauce
8 ounces squid rings (about 2 cups)

# Italian-Style Stewed Bell Peppers (*Peperonata*)

6 SERVINGS

Bell peppers stewed in a fresh tomato sauce is a common vegetable dish in Italy, but here in New Jersey, it is served more often as a condiment. You can use it in many other ways though: as a warm appetizer, a sauce for pasta, potatoes, or rice, or even as a vegetarian main course.

Heat the oil with the anchovies in a large pot over low heat and stir gently until the anchovies disintegrate. Add the garlic, seasoning, and salt and cook, stirring until the garlic becomes a bit translucent. Add the onion and continue cooking over low heat until tender. Add the tomatoes and continue cooking, stirring frequently. When the tomatoes are well cooked, about 15 minutes, add the bell peppers, stirring to coat with the tomato mixture. Simmer for another 30 or 40 minutes, until the peppers are tender and the flavors have blended. Serve immediately.

2 tablespoons olive oil
3 anchovy fillets
3 cloves garlic, chopped
1½ teaspoons Italian seasoning
1 teaspoon salt
1 medium onion, chopped
  (about 1 cup)
3 tomatoes, chopped
  (about 3 cups)
4 bell peppers, cut into
  1-inch squares
½ teaspoon freshly ground
  black pepper

# Stokes Farm

Old Tappan, BERGEN COUNTY

Only twenty-seven miles from Manhattan, you can't really call a farm "rural." If doctor's offices and fine-dining restaurants are within walking distance, there is a whole different sense of a farm's role in a neighborhood. Stokes Farm in Old Tappan is in just this sort of location, but unlike Abma's Farm Market, which has a sophisticated on-site retail operation, Stokes does most of its selling away from home. They're regulars at New York City's Greenmarkets, in fact they were among the original twelve farms that sold there.

Old Tappan, the Bergen County town where Stokes Farm is located, could be called "commuter country" and Ron Binaghi, Jr., the fifth-generation owner, could certainly be described as a commuter. At least three days a week, he can be found in New York City, selling herbs, eggplants, heirloom tomatoes, broccoli, and peppers.

The farm itself is well hidden from the main road. Driving by, you'll see the stand, garden center, and the Binaghi family home. However, to get a good look at the fields and greenhouses, you'll have to head up a hard-to-find driveway. There, a red barn—Manhattan is said to be visible from its roof—marks the top of a knoll where twelve acres of herbs and five of vegetables slope down towards office buildings and townhouses. Long rows of double poly greenhouses finish the scene, extending the Stokes growing season by several months. This gives them produce both many weeks earlier and later than their competitors, and an edge at the markets.

Isaiah Stokes founded Stokes Farm in 1873. His granddaughter inherited the place and married a Binaghi in 1927. Three generations, including her son, work the farm today. But there is recent history too: Ron remembers the first Manhattan Greenmarket at 59th Street and Second Avenue back in 1976. He was a teenager and his family grew nothing but tomatoes, peppers, eggplants, and strawberries. Back in those days, Greenmarket customers were kept behind a fence until the market officially opened. When the moment came, the seething crowd overwhelmed them, buying everything they could and often clearing out their truck in only a few hours.

Things are different today. The crowds are calmer, but they are far more demanding. "We have to be savvy by default," Ron says. He speaks of the fierce competition between vendors. "We're always under the magnifying glass." The Greenmarket presents farmers with a dilemma: If they can grow something better tasting or more interesting than the other guy, they can then sell it for a price that many farmers can only dream of. If they can't, they'll be unable to even stay in business.

Best of all, when the farmers succeed, they earn a remarkable amount of respect from those consumers. "Our customers are powerful people, and the cool thing is that they think we're cool! I went to the James Beard dinner and guests had to pay extra for sitting with farmers. They just wanted to know what I did," enthuses Ron. For city people, there is a certain comfort in knowing where your food comes from and meeting the person who produced it.

Walking through the fields and greenhouses here, nothing is ever described generally. There is no "basil" growing at Stokes Farm, but there is "Thai basil" and "Opal basil." It's the same with tomatoes. No generic tomatoes grow here, but at least six types of heirlooms do. Nine kinds of eggplant. Small Thai varieties, big purple ones, even eggplants that are red or green.

There is always some pressure from developers, but Ron manages to keep ahead in several different ways. He's a member of the town council, an avid reader, and one of those people who's always up on news and business. In conversation, he'd rather talk about Wall Street or English football ("my addiction") than farming, but when the topic is agriculture he can certainly hold his own. Asked about the future, he says, "You never hear anybody say, 'Hey! They ripped the mall down and put up a farm!'" But then again, he's not talking to any mall developers.

# Roasted Potato Salad

4 SERVINGS

Potatoes are millions of people's favorite food, but bringing the best out of them takes a bit of skill. Luckily for us, in New Jersey we have plenty of inspiration. Potato salad is a favorite and the state is filled with variations on the theme. This recipe is for what many of us called "German" potato salad, but it is a bit modernized with roasted potatoes, olive oil, and wine vinegar. The dish is best either slightly warm or at room temperature, but you can serve it chilled too.

Preheat the oven to 425°F.

Put the potatoes on a nonstick baking sheet and spread the bacon over them evenly. Season with salt and pepper and bake for 40 minutes, or until the potatoes are tender. Remove the pan from the oven and let cool.

Then place the potatoes in a bowl along with the peppers, oil, and vinegar. Toss until all the ingredients are well mixed. Let stand for at least 1 hour at room temperature (or longer in the refrigerator) before serving to allow the potatoes to absorb the other flavors.

2 pounds potatoes, cut into 1-inch pieces
4 ounces bacon, cut into small strips
Salt
Freshly ground black pepper
1 large red or yellow bell pepper, cut into strips
3 tablespoons olive oil
2 tablespoons white wine vinegar

# Stewed Calamari with Potatoes

4 SERVINGS

This is a cross between two Italian classics: one from the deep south using fresh tomatoes and a Tuscan dish with potatoes. It also has chile peppers thrown in for a bit of extra kick.

Heat the oil in a heavy soup pot over low heat. Add the anchovies and stir gently until they disintegrate. Add the garlic, chile, and seasoning, making sure they're coated well with the anchovy mixture. Turn the heat up to medium-low and add the onion and squid. Cook until the squid is opaque. (The squid will be quite tough at this point, but it will become tender again as it cooks.) Now add the potatoes, tomatoes, and bell peppers, give them a few good stirs, and add the wine. Bring the mixture to a simmer, stirring occasionally, for about 1 hour, or until the squid is tender and the potatoes are soft.

* Habanero and jalapeño will both work; chipotle will add a smoky twist.

** Red new or Yukon Gold potatoes are my favorite varieties, but feel free to experiment.

1 tablespoon olive oil
4 anchovy fillets
6 cloves garlic, chopped
1 chile pepper, chopped*
1 tablespoon Italian seasoning
1 large onion, chopped
1½ pounds cleaned squid, cut into rings
3 medium potatoes, cubed (about 1 pound)**
3 tomatoes, chopped (about 2 cups)
1 red or yellow bell pepper, cut into 1-inch squares
2 cups dry white wine

# Curried Baked Squash

4 SERVINGS

This dish isn't a curry in the authentic Asian sense; it's not something that people in Thailand or India eat. But it's an interesting way to season pumpkins or winter squash and a different way to use curry paste.

Heat the oil and curry paste in a medium skillet over low heat and mix until combined. Add the onion and cook, stirring until it is very tender and the curry paste and oil are completely absorbed. Add the squash and continue cooking, stirring occasionally for about 20 minutes. Taste to see if it needs salt and pepper. When that's done, it's ready to serve.

* Butternut squash works best, but in a pinch, almost any pumpkin will do. Be aware that those big orange ones take a long time to bake!

**SERVING NOTE:** Reheat in the microwave if the mixture has cooled down too much. In fact, the dish will benefit from a bit of time standing in the refrigerator.

2 tablespoons vegetable oil
2 tablespoons mild curry paste
1 medium onion, chopped
   (about 1 cup)
3 cups cooked fresh pumpkin
   (or two 10-ounce packages
   frozen squash)
Salt
Freshly ground black pepper

# Sweet Potato Gnocchi

4 SERVINGS

Gnocchi are a pasta traditionally made with white potato and flour. Here's a New World variation that substitutes sweet potatoes.

Preheat the oven to 400°F. Roast the sweet potatoes until soft, about 40 minutes. Set aside until cool enough to handle.

Peel the potatoes into a large bowl (you should have about 1 cup of mashed potatoes). Add the egg, salt, and nutmeg and mash. Add the flour a spoonful at a time and work it into the mixture until it becomes a dough.

Roll the dough into ropes, and cut them into 1-inch pieces. Lightly press them with the back of a fork; this gives them ribs like little seashells and helps the sauce to stick.

To cook them, bring a pot of salted water to a boil and add the gnocchi. They will sink to the bottom at first but they'll soon float to the top. Cook them for 12 minutes timed from the moment they float. Drain and serve with butter and grated Parmesan or Romano cheese.

For a non-dairy alternative, serve the gnocchi with walnut oil, salt, and pepper.

1 pound sweet potatoes
1 large egg
1 teaspoon salt
½ teaspoon ground nutmeg
1½ cups whole wheat flour
Butter for serving
Parmesan or Romano cheese
   for serving

# Basic Tomato Sauce

YIELDS 1 QUART; 6 TO 8 SERVINGS

In both Italy and in New Jersey, basic tomato sauce skills are a metric of kitchen prowess. This recipe could be the beginning of a seduction or the prelude to a divorce. When you have a supply of this sauce in your freezer, you are ready for anything. Use it by itself on pasta, over whole fish, or with vegetables. Serious cooks make this in large quantities at harvest time and can or freeze it.

Heat the oil in a large pot over low heat and add the carrot, garlic, and seasoning. Sauté until the garlic is translucent. Add the onion and continue cooking until the onions are translucent. Turn the heat up to medium and add the tomatoes, salt, and pepper. Simmer for about 30 minutes, stirring occasionally. Let the mixture cool.

Pass the sauce through a food mill or processor in small batches. Choose the disk that matches your cooking style. Small for a very refined sauce, large for a coarser and more robust one. If you use a food processor, you can process the whole recipe in one batch.

2 tablespoons olive oil
1 carrot, peeled and chopped
4 cloves garlic, chopped
2 tablespoons Italian seasoning
1 medium onion, chopped
    (about 1 cup)
3 pounds plum tomatoes,
    quartered
1 ½ teaspoons salt
1 teaspoon freshly ground black
    pepper

To freeze, pour the sauce into wide-mouth freezer and microwave safe containers until they are about three quarters full. Cover and place in an uncrowded section of the freezer. At first, they'll need the cold air circulating around them, but after a day or so, they can be stacked in a corner. Make sure you clearly label every container with the contents and date of preparation. Kept this way, the sauce will last 4-6 months.

**NOTE:** Don't hesitate to personalize your sauce. There are zillions of possible variations! I've tried 2 to 3 tablespoons of olive paste, a few anchovies, and a bit of potato. Each of these additions will make your sauce a bit unique.

# Penne in Spicy Tomato Sauce (*Penne alla Arrabiata*)

4 SERVINGS

Spicy pasta dishes are often included on New Jersey Italian menus. This one, a fairly classic recipe, is always a hit. *Arrabiata* means "angry" in Italian, but it's a pleasure for spicy food lovers.

Make the sauce: In a skillet large enough to hold both the pasta and the sauce, heat the oil. Add the anchovies, seasoning, and salt and cook, stirring over low heat until the anchovies disintegrate. Add the garlic and peppers and keep cooking until the garlic becomes a bit translucent. Turn the heat up to medium and add the tomatoes, stirring, until the tomatoes are coated with the oil mixture, and bring to a simmer. The sauce will be ready for pasta with as little as 15 minutes of simmering but will continue to improve for at least another 15 or 20 minutes.

1 tablespoon olive oil
4 anchovy fillets
1 tablespoon Italian seasoning
1 teaspoon salt, plus extra for water
4 cloves garlic, chopped
2 small chile peppers, chopped
4 tomatoes, chopped (about 3 cups)
1 pound penne pasta

While the sauce is cooking, bring a large pot of salted water to a boil and cook the pasta for about 1 minute less than the package indicates. Drain and add to the sauce. Simmer the pasta and sauce for about 1 minute, stirring constantly, making sure that the pasta is evenly coated with the sauce. Serve.

# Watershed Organic Farm CSA

The Stony Brook–Millstone Watershed Association owns over 700 acres of land in western Mercer County. They have a nature center, eight miles of hiking trails, a fishing pond, picnic tables, and a ninety-acre working organic farm called Watershed Organic Farm CSA. People often bring lawn chairs with them when they visit and it's a pleasant place to go and spend an afternoon.

Jim Kinsel, the farm's manager, feels that this is an important selling point. For example, in the days following the September 11 attacks, he worked hard to make Watershed a place of quiet contemplation and people just found themselves coming there and comforting each other. Even when there isn't tragedy in the air, Watershed's regulars will sit out front watching crops being picked and machinery being repaired. Jim sees this as a strange twist in the world of agri-tainment—

unlike those farms that have petting zoos, blow-up dolls of carrots, hayrides, or musicians, Watershed just farms and people gather and watch. For many, it's just as much about belonging. Sherry Dudas, the farm's resident planner, says that it's the equivalent of a coffee shop where people go to meet and socialize.

Organic farms are often criticized for high prices, but the CSA model really brings costs down. Of course, this doesn't stop their well-off neighbors from joining—they get the same box as everybody else. All wind up with fresh, organic produce for about sixty percent of the retail price.

The farm was started by the Watershed Association in the mid-1980s to demonstrate the viability of sustainable farming practices. And within a few years, people were growing great things here. The farmer before Jim was Helen Atthowe, now an author of gardening books who lives in Montana. It was at Watershed that she pioneered moving techniques like staking and growing under plastic from the home garden to the farm field. Her tomatoes won awards that put the farm on the map.

Jim and a friend came to the farm twelve years ago. They shared the work and profits equally and at the end of that first year, sat down to assess the situation. His friend thought the whole thing was a failure and left, but Jim was delighted; he wasn't starving, had a roof over his head, and knew where his food was coming from. It was a complete success from his point of view.

Choosing what crops a CSA grows is very different than planning for the retail market. Those farmers put on a show. They know that drawing big crowds is a key to success, but at Watershed, the problem is keeping the contents of the boxes interesting enough so that members don't give up and go to the supermarket and predictable enough to calm those with less wide-ranging tastes. This means that not everybody is going to be pleased. Beets are too exotic for some members and kohlrabi is too dull for others.

Because of these complaints, Jim has deviated from the standard CSA model and is now adapting one based on methods used at Food Bank Farm in Hadley, MA. This way, some of the contents are dictated and the rest is broken up into "choice groups" that members can select from during visits. This means that Jim and Sherry wind up growing everything from arugula to zucchini with one big exception: sweet corn. The soil at Watershed just isn't suited to it. Melons and cucumbers present the most difficulties. They work hard on pest management solutions for these crops and find better methods as the years go by.

Besides the satisfaction of farming for their 2,600 member/customers, Jim also finds a certain inspiration in being near the city. He and Sherry could get a place five times larger in a nice quiet corner of rural America and farm in peace, but there is something about being this close to New York and Philadelphia that challenges him. "I think I belong here," he says. "I want to stay and fight."

# Stewed Heirloom Tomatoes

4 SERVINGS

It's time to admit the truth: You've bought far too many heirloom tomatoes to eat in salads, sandwiches, or any other raw way. They are getting riper and riper by the day and despite their incredible colors, you can't stand to look at them anymore.

People spend too much time wondering what to do in situations like this. The unwritten rule book says to never cook heirloom tomatoes, but it also seems foolish to trash them. This recipe is based on an idea from the folks at Peaceful Valley Orchards (page 188) and really seems to benefit from the use of heirloom tomatoes.

Heat the oil in a soup pot over medium heat and add the garlic, bacon, seasoning, salt, and pepper. When the garlic starts to become translucent, add the onion and pepper and keep cooking over medium heat until the onions are soft. Stir in the tomatoes and lower the heat. Soon the tomatoes will give off liquid and the pot will start to simmer. Cook, uncovered, stirring occasionally, for about 20 minutes, until the tomatoes start to brown, and serve.

2 tablespoons olive oil
4 cloves garlic, cut into chunks
1 slice bacon, cut into slivers
1 tablespoon Italian seasoning
1½ teaspoons salt
1½ teaspoons freshly ground
   black pepper
1 medium onion, chopped
   (about 1 cup)
1 bell pepper, cut into bite-size
   pieces (about 1 cup)
4 really ripe heirloom tomatoes,
   quartered

# Gazpacho

4 SERVINGS

Many American recipes for this soup tend to push it towards Mexico with the addition of garlic, chile, herbs, or other Latin ingredients, but in Spain, this is a mildly sweet and refreshing drink that's often served in bars alongside coffee and wine. Think of it as a liquid way to get the recalcitrant to eat their salad. As Spanish as it is though, you can't help but notice that it's a mixture of some of New Jersey's favorite crops.

Put the tomatoes, broth, salt, and pepper in a blender and liquefy, about 1 minute. Add the cucumber, carrot, and bell pepper and continue blending until the contents are puréed, about 2 more minutes (old blenders can take a bit longer). Serve chilled.

4 ripe tomatoes, chopped
   (about 2 cups)
1 cup vegetable broth
1 teaspoon salt
½ teaspoon freshly ground
   black pepper
1 large cucumber, chopped
   (about 1 cup)
2 medium carrots, peeled and
   chopped (about 1 cup)
1 red or yellow bell pepper,
   chopped (about 1 cup)

# Baked Green Tomatoes

4 SERVINGS

Fried green tomatoes are a classic southern dish and the name of a beloved book and film. While the idea of fried green tomatoes is a good one, it presents a big problem in practice— they are fried. How can green tomatoes, that farm market favorite, be served without making a greasy mess? Why not just season them and bake them? After all, there is oven-fried chicken.

Preheat the oven to 400°F and grease a baking sheet with olive oil. Place the green tomato slices on the baking sheet. Combine the seasoning and garlic salt. Dust the tomatoes with this mixture. Bake for 25 minutes, until tender, and serve immediately as a vegetable side.

1½ pounds green tomatoes, cut into ½-inch-thick slices
2 tablespoons Italian seasoning
1 tablespoon garlic salt*

* Try "Alho & Sal," a Brazilian product found in most Portuguese markets.

# Tuscan Bread and Tomato Salad (*Panzanella*)

154

6 SERVINGS

This is a classic bread salad from central Italy that finds its way into thousands of New Jersey homes during the tomato season. When you're making this dish, feel free to use any kind of bread you have around. Any bread worth eating will taste good in the salad.

Mix all of the ingredient together in a large bowl and toss until they're well combined. Cover and place in the refrigerator for at least 8 hours before serving. The dish will continue to improve for several days.

**VARIATIONS:** Popular additions to this dish include chopped cucumbers, bell pepper strips, capers, and anchovies. Less traditional, but equally good are canned tuna and chile peppers.

2 cups bite-size pieces stale bread
2 fresh tomatoes, chopped (about 2 cups)
1 small red onion, minced
½ cup chopped fresh Italian parsley
¼ cup olive oil
2 cloves garlic, chopped
2 tablespoons red wine vinegar
2 teaspoons salt
1 teaspoon freshly ground black pepper

# Heirloom Tomato and Peach Salsa

YIELD 5 CUPS

Combining a trip to the farm stands of central New Jersey with a stop at a local Mexican market, the idea of blending heirloom tomato salsa with classic Mexican ingredients came to mind. If you're the chip eating sort, you can serve this with them, but in a pinch—and there's always a pinch—this can go on burgers, fish, or even elbow macaroni for a spicy pasta salad.

Combine all of the ingredients in a large bowl and mix well. Let the salsa sit for 10 or 15 minutes and mix again. Refrigerate for at least 6 hours before serving to allow the flavors to combine.

**N O T E :** You can adjust the heat by adding more or less garlic and/or chipotles, and the sweetness by adding more fruit.

1 large heirloom tomato, chopped (about 2 cups)
1 large red onion, chopped
1 red or yellow bell pepper, chopped (about 1 cup)
1 ripe peach, pitted and chopped
3 cloves garlic, chopped
3 canned chipotle peppers, chopped (Be careful here! They're hot.)
3 tablespoons cider vinegar
1½ teaspoons salt
Freshly ground black pepper

# Chia-Sin Farms

Pittstown, Hunterdon County

Driving down a small country road in west central New Jersey, you'll notice a garden center that looks pretty typical, but if you give it a second glance, you'll see that the entrance is marked in Chinese characters. This alone is enough to arouse many people's curiosity, but Chia-Sin Farms is well known to serious fans of Asian gardens and horticulture.

This is one of New Jersey's great Asian food outposts. Located in Pittstown, near exit 15 of I-78, it's deep in farm country, but not really that far from suburbia. It's less than an hour from the Asian communities of Edison, Highland Park, and South Plainfield and two hours from Manhattan.

There is a lot here that makes this farm similar to many others. Row after row of houseplants and bins of tomatoes. But when you look more closely, you see that the plants are named in both English and Chinese. In fact, as you move deeper into the property, the English starts vanishing.

In his "office," a picnic table in front of the chicken coop at the edge of the cabbage and squash field, owner Charlie Wong talks enthusiastically about his farm. A small and powerfully built man with a big smile, he has a well-worn leather cowboy hat and the sort of deeply tanned face that speaks of long days outdoors.

Charlie Wong came to New Jersey from Taiwan in 1976 to work for an orchid grower in Clinton. Over the years, both the state's Asian population and the general public's interest in Asian foods, plants, and flowers grew rapidly. In 1991 he bought Chia Sin Farms, and started growing Taiwanese cabbage, okra, bitter melons, chile peppers, Chinese squashes, sweet potato greens, and a large selection of Asian sweet melons.

For Charlie, the biggest issue has always been getting the word out. He advertises in Chinese newspapers, and even places an occasional commercial on local Chinese-language TV. The result is that customers from Virginia to Boston know him as the place to go for Asian specialties.

In the beginning, the problem wasn't quality but credibility. Nobody was ready to believe that a farm only sixty miles from the Empire State Building was growing produce rarely seen in North America. But when word started getting around, Chia-Sin was ready for the crowds. Busloads of people came from the big city, and they've never stopped.

Charlie isn't just excited by farming, he's a food enthusiast of the first degree. He travels all over the state seeking out great restaurants. His specialty is the food of his native Taiwan and he raves about a place on Route 27 in Kendall Park. He regularly drives there for "the real stuff…the real food of Taiwan, not sweet like Shanghai or spicy like Szechuan." This is an eighty-mile round-trip. But the look in his eyes told me that he wouldn't care if it was ten times farther.

At home, he and his family aren't big meat eaters. They sometimes eat the Chinese variety free-range chickens they keep, but they mostly cook with the vegetables they grow themselves. His first choice is yam greens and his favorite way of cooking them is to stir-fry them in olive oil. Not very authentic, but a good New Jersey combination! He is also fond of the Chinese classic, stir-fried eggs with tomatoes (page 67). He is proud to say that it tastes far better with the ingredients he produces himself on the farm.

If you walk with Charlie through his fields, he'll stop and show you how beautiful his yam greens are, how great his bitter melons look, and how wonderful his Taiwanese cabbages taste. You can sense his enthusiasm as he pulls out his folding knife and cuts a sample to taste. His final words? "You don't do this for money."

# Stir-Fried Yam Leaves

4 SERVINGS

Yam leaves are a popular Chinese green, similar to spinach. As Charlie picked them, he described his favorite stir-fry method. Who would expect the combination of olive oil and soy sauce to work? But work it did.

Heat a wok on your hottest burner over high heat. Add the oil and give it a minute to heat up. Carefully put in the garlic and soy sauce and stir. You should see some serious sizzling action. Add the greens in fistfuls. They will shrink rapidly and within a few moments there will be room in the pan for all the greens. Keep stirring—they don't call this "stir-frying" for nothing! The greens will continue to shrink. It's ready when the stems are as tender as well-cooked broccoli, about 5 minutes.

**3 tablespoons olive oil**
**6 cloves garlic, smashed**
**3 tablespoons soy sauce**
**8 cups yam leaves**

**NOTE:** This recipe will work well with any of the vegetable shoots sold in Chinese markets. Of course, none of them taste as good as Charlie's yam leaves.

# Zucchini Marinated in Vinegar and Wine (*Zucchini in Carpione*)

4 SERVINGS

Perfect for making ahead of time and serving straight from the fridge. *Zucchini in carpione* is a hot summer's day favorite from the north of Italy. Of course, it's one more thing you can do with all those zucchini.

Heat the oil in a large skillet over a medium flame and brown the zucchini. Drain the zucchini and blot with paper towels to absorb excess oil. Set it aside and reserve the oil in the pan. Sauté the onions and garlic in the same oil. When they become translucent, add the sage, vinegar, wine, pepper, allspice, and bay leaves and cook for 4 minutes on high heat, until the flavors have combined.

Lay the zucchini flat in a nonmetal container. Layer the onions evenly on top of the zucchini, and refrigerate for 5 to 6 hours.

**NOTE:** For a lowfat version, grill or broil the zucchini slices instead of frying them. Use just 1 tablespoon oil for the onions.

½ cup olive oil
1 pound zucchini, thinly sliced lengthwise
1 large white onion, thinly sliced
2 garlic cloves, thinly sliced
4 bunches fresh sage, chopped
1 cup white wine vinegar
½ cup dry white wine
2 teaspoons whole black peppercorns
1 teaspoon whole allspice
3 bay leaves

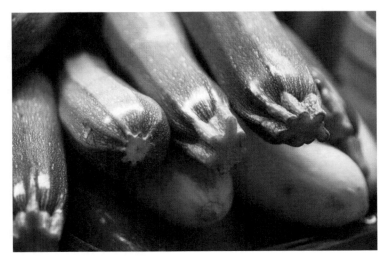

# J.C. Hazlett Farm
# and Market

Goshen, CAPE MAY COUNTY

Cape May County is as far south as you can be in New Jersey. If you're driving down from Bergen or Passaic in the middle of the winter, you feel the air getting warmer as you approach. In the roadside shops and cafés, locals speak with more than a touch of a southern accent. But this is still part of the Garden State. This is where you'll find J.C. Hazlett Farm and Market.

Tucked in between the pine forests of the interior and the wetlands of Delaware Bay, the farm is one of many along Route 47. It's set in a bit from the road and takes some searching to find. But Jim Hazlett, the farm's owner, says, "We're in the chicken coop," and he means it. When he bought the property back in 1981, the only structure on it was that coop, so he converted the feed storage area into a bedroom of sorts and he gradually improved it over the years. Today, you see a beautiful home with bits of chicken coop sticking out the sides, a comfortable residence with slightly odd dimensions.

The farm is owned and run by Jim and Carol Hazlett. Both have the fit, tanned look of people who happily spend their lives outdoors. Jim, with his graying beard and sparkling eyes, is the very picture of a small farmer. Carol, with her cheerful smile, looks no less the part. Neither of them have any real vegetable farming background. Jim was a suburbanite to the core and Carol grew up in Glassboro, an industrial town. Having worked on a dairy farm before, Jim knew from the first moment he could make a go of the chicken coop.

Twenty-five years ago, organic was an alien concept and vegetables either came from a supermarket, home garden, or a frozen package. But Jim and Carol have been growing without chemicals from the beginning. Soon the word got around and people began to buy. Now, Cape May is a major weekend and retirement destination and the Hazlett's food is sought out as a quality local product.

Things have come a long way. A state agriculture agent is supportive and enthusiastic and many other local farmers are starting to adopt organic techniques even if only to cut down on the sky-rocketing cost of chemicals. Jim reminds us, "I'm not in debt because I don't buy fertilizer. In fact, not many salesmen come to the farm anymore." On the other hand, he also says, "The American consumer isn't ready to have their whole diet organic; they're not yet prepared to pick up an ear of corn and find a worm—and in order to keep the worm out, you've got to spray it."

This is a classic vegetable farm—a twenty-acre market garden in the Garden State. There are time-honored Jersey crops like lima beans, peas, spinach, and beets. Also newer items like Asian egg-plants, tomatillos, yellow watermelons, and the ever popular heirloom tomatoes. In fact, years before the Victorian homes were a major tourist destination, the Lima Bean Festival was one of Cape May's major events.

Hazlett's isn't the easiest place to find out about. They never advertise and depend on word of mouth, showing up at the local farmer's market and in brochures put out by the Northeast Organic Farming Association. Jim would like to hook up with some of the fine-dining restaurants that are springing up around Cape May, but it hasn't happened yet. They are also starting a CSA, the first in this part of the state. (See Watershed Organic Farm, page 149 for more information on CSAs.)

Jim and Carol thrive on the challenge of farming. "Every day's different. Nothing ever goes as planned," Jim reminds us. Of course their location, on a narrow strip of land between Delaware Bay and the Atlantic Ocean, makes the weather very fickle and unpredictable. But life is good here. As Carol says while pointing to an old photo of Jim in their scrapbook, "Good, because he made it good."

# Pasta Primavera

4 SERVINGS

*Primavera* means spring in Italian. When you can find asparagus and zucchini at local markets, you'll know that winter is really over. This sauce works well with many different pasta shapes. I like it with *penne* and my wife prefers *orecchiette*. Others swear by *fusilli*, *gemelli*, or even *strozza-preti*. If you're not confident in your Italian, just think anything round and fat.

Heat the oil over low heat in a large skillet. Add the garlic and seasoning, and sauté until lightly browned. Add the onion and cook until translucent. Next, raise the heat to medium-low, put in the bell peppers, asparagus, mushrooms, and zucchini and sauté for 5 more minutes. Finally, mix in the tomatoes and simmer for 15 minutes. Add the salt and pepper and serve with grated cheese.

2 tablespoons olive oil
3 cloves garlic, chopped
1 tablespoon Italian seasoning
1 large onion, chopped
1 bell pepper, cut into strips
4 ounces asparagus spears, chopped (about ½ cup)
2 ounces chopped fresh mushrooms (about ½ cup)
1 small zucchini, chopped (about ½ cup)
1 (28-ounce) can unpeeled crushed tomatoes
1 teaspoon salt
1 teaspoon freshly ground black pepper
Grated cheese for serving

# Thai-Style Vegetable Salad

4 SERVINGS

Thai dressings are a refreshing change from the usual bottled dressings, especially for those people who want serious spiciness in every place they can find it. This recipe differs from authentic Thai in one major way: Its main ingredients are all grown or (in the case of bean sprouts) produced in New Jersey.

To make the dressing: Mix the lime juice, fish sauce, sugar, and garlic in a sealable container and let stand for at least 1 hour.

Combine the salad ingredients in a large bowl and toss with the dressing. Serve immediately. If the salad sits too long, the acid in the dressing will "cook" the vegetables.

## DRESSING
¼ cup lime juice
3 tablespoons fish sauce
1 tablespoon palm or raw sugar
1 clove garlic, chopped

## SALAD
1 cup arugula
1 cup mung bean sprouts
1 cup (½ pint) grape tomatoes
1 small bell pepper, cut into
  strips
1 medium apple, cored and
  chopped (about ½ cup)

# FRUIT

166

# FRUIT

In even the most urban neighborhoods in New Jersey, one finds "Grove Streets" and "Vineyard Lanes." There are clues to the state's history as a fruit producer all over. Apples, peaches, and pears flourish here and orchards are found in every part of the state. Berries are big too; the cranberry of course—it's native and grows wild in the Pine Barrens—but you'll also find blueberries, strawberries, and raspberries.

Unlike most of the other farm products you see, fruit is often eaten raw. But for moments when those apples, peaches, pears, or cranberries demand that they be turned into a special treat, here are some recipes.

# Apple Dumplings

4 SERVINGS

This dish seems to have snuck into New Jersey from Pennsylvania and is popular on both sides of the river. Try serving a dumpling in a bowl with warm milk poured over it. A soothing dessert if there ever was one.

Preheat the oven to 350°F. Grease a baking sheet.

2 tablespoons sugar
1 teaspoon ground cinnamon
1 teaspoon ground nutmeg
2 apples, peeled, cored, and halved
1 batch piecrust dough (see page 193 or 194)*

Mix the sugar, cinnamon, and nutmeg together and sprinkle it over the apples.

Cut the piecrust into squares large enough to wrap each apple half. Put the dough on a flat surface, place an apple half in the middle, and fold the dough so it wraps around the fruit and bring it together at the top. Pinch the dough at the edges to make sure the package is sealed. Place on a greased baking sheet and bake for 45 minutes, or until the crust is well browned. Serve plain, with warm milk (Amish-Style), or with ice cream.

* You can buy and use a premade piecrust here, nobody will tell on you! Just make sure you buy the kind that doesn't already come frozen and in a pie pan.

# Poached Asian Pears in Cranberry Sauce

4 SERVINGS

Asian Pears look like giant golden apples and are often offered in fancy netting or tissue wrapping. In this fall recipe, they are cooked with cranberries and spices as a simple fruit dessert. Or, serve as a fruit course at any meal. It's even good with morning breakfast cereal.

Bring 3 cups water to a boil in a sauce pan and add the cranberries, sugar, cloves, and cardamom. Reduce the heat and simmer for 5 minutes. Add the pears. Simmer for 15 minutes, stirring occasionally, until the pears are tender and the cranberries have burst.

**4 ounces fresh cranberries (1 cup)**
**½ cup packed brown sugar**
**3 whole cloves**
**1 cardamom pod**
**3 Asian pears, cut into bite-size pieces (about 2 cups)**

# Asian Pear Pie

6 TO 8 SERVINGS

Asian pears are a bit too luxurious to put in pies very often, but out at places like Chia-Sin Farm (page 156), you can often find a sack of Asian pears at a reasonable price. Combine them with a bit of Chinese five-spice and you have a unique, delicious pie.

Preheat the oven to 350°F.

Fit the bottom crust into a 9-inch pie pan.

Mix the pears, sugar, five-spice, and lemon juice together in a large bowl. Be sure that all the fruit is evenly coated. Pour the fruit into the bottom crust and cover it with the top crust. Make a few slits in the top crust for the steam to escape. Bake the pie for 40 minutes, until the fruit is soft and the crust is golden brown. Allow it to cool for 10 minutes before serving.

1 recipe piecrust dough
  (page 193 or 194)
6 to 8 Asian pears, peeled, cored,
  and sliced (6 cups)
½ cup sugar
1 tablespoon five-spice powder
1 teaspoon lemon juice

# Big Buck Farms

Hammonton, ATLANTIC COUNTY

Are they growing red sticks around here? Well, that's what you might think driving the back roads around Atlantic County. Huge fields covered with small dark bushes as far as the eye can see. But for a few short months, from the end of May through the beginning of August, these fields are alive with activity. They are New Jersey's blueberry farms, the most productive source of fresh blueberries in the nation. Other states might do better with fruit for pie filling or jam, but when it comes to those beautiful, small trays you see in fancy markets, this area leads the way.

Big Buck Farms, owned by Louis Condo, is one such holding. With 120 acres of blueberries, fifty-two of them certified organic, it's a bit too small to be thought of as a factory farm and a bit too large to do the sort of tailgate retail marketing that works for smaller operations. Still, Louis is thriving and his methods and outlook are worth noting.

Big Buck Farms is home to…well…big bucks. It's on the edge of the flat, sandy-soiled pine forests that dominate the center of the state. This, along with slow moving, marsh-like rivers, makes a habitat perfect for both deer and blueberries.

Although there are farmers in Louis's family tree, he wasn't born on a farm. He worked in construction and at a gas station and was looking for something with more stability when he was offered the chance to farm on leased land eight years ago. He liked it, bought his own property, and that's what he's been doing ever since.

As a crop, as a business, and as a food, Louis and his family love blueberries. They're perennials; that is, they don't have to be replanted every year. "You don't need much: your tractor, your sprayer, and that's about it," he says. They have an annual ritual that has become the calendar of their life. April has its weeding and weed spraying. In May, the first flowers break and the fertilizing begins. By the end of June, there are often sixty or more temporary employees harvesting and that lasts through July. As August begins, the season ends with machines that go over the bushes for anything the more careful hand pickings have missed. These leftovers can be sold in bulk to processors, but they aren't what Big Buck Farms is all about.

Business-wise, Louis's goal is to produce the highest quality fresh packed berries possible. Sold in half-pint trays in fine stores, they must be very selective. With over forty percent of his land certified organic and possessing a sharp eye for defects, Louis is able to attract high-end distributors like Jersey Fruit and Albert's and command solid prices for his product.

Asked about their own taste in food, Louis's wife Liz, the farm's bookkeeper and quality control person begins enumerating some of the ways the family eats blueberries. Of course, they make jam, muffins, and pancakes, but they also make blueberry wine and brandy for their own use. (For commercial sources of New Jersey blueberry wine see Bellview Winery, page 14, or Tomasello Winery, page 10.)

Scratch the surface of almost any southern New Jersey farm family and you'll find an astounding repository of European immigrant foodways. Italian-American–style Sunday gravy at mom's might be a legend in much of this country, but it's reality for the Condo family. As he raves about mom's meatballs, he leaves the room and comes back with the sort of dried salami that is a rare treat for most of us. Mildly spiced, but redolent of fennel, it provides the perfect backdrop for a discussion of Louis's favorites. Of course, Louis makes it himself from a family recipe and uses locally produced and butchered pork.

So why do they do it? Louis Condo isn't the sort of idealist one might imagine as a modern farmer, and while he may be able to earn a decent living and shoot a bit of venison on his property, he isn't in it for the money. But when asked, his reply is quick: "We have the best organic blueberries around!"

# Blueberry-Walnut Loaf

1 LOAF; 10 TO 12 SERVINGS

This breakfast bread is easy to make and is always a big hit. Make it instead of pancakes or French toast, or as a snack or dessert.

Preheat the oven to 400°F and grease a 9x5-inch loaf pan.

Blend the flour, baking powder, and salt together in a large bowl and then mix in the sugar, oil, egg, cinnamon, and nutmeg with 1 cup water. You should have a thick batter at this point. Now mix in the blueberries and walnut pieces. Pour the contents into the prepared pan and bake for 1 hour, until the top springs back when touched. Cool in the pan for 5 to 10 minutes, then unmold to cool completely, and serve.

1½ cups sifted all-purpose flour
1 tablespoon baking powder
½ teaspoon salt
¾ cup packed brown or raw sugar
½ cup vegetable oil
1 egg, lightly beaten
1 teaspoon ground cinnamon
½ teaspoon ground nutmeg
4 ounces blueberries (1 cup)
4 ounces walnut pieces (1 cup)

# Whole Wheat Blueberry-Apple Muffins

8 MUFFINS

There's nothing like a great home-baked muffin for breakfast in the morning. These use classic New Jersey ingredients: blueberries and apples and are whole grain too.

Preheat the oven to 450°F and spray a muffin pan with cooking spray.

Combine the flours, blueberries, apple, baking powder, and salt in a bowl. Make sure they are well combined. A few stirs with a whisk usually do the job. Now add the milk, honey, molasses, egg, and butter and stir a few more times. It's better to have a few lumps than to overmix. Pour the batter into the muffin pan; the cups should be about two-thirds full. Bake for 20 minutes, until the tops spring back when lightly touched. Cool slightly and serve.

1½ cups sifted whole wheat flour
⅔ cup sifted all-purpose flour
2 ounces fresh blueberries (about ½ cup)
1 medium apple, cored and chopped (½ cup)
2 teaspoons baking powder
1 teaspoon salt
1½ cups milk or soy milk
3 tablespoons honey
2 tablespoons molasses
1 egg, lightly beaten
1 tablespoon butter, melted

# Terhune Orchards

The first things you notice about Terhune Orchards are the scarecrows. Birds and deer may find them frightening, but to visitors looking for fruit and vegetables, they're a warm welcome. There's also plenty of parking here, so you don't have to worry about showing up at the height of the harvest season and not being able to get out of your car. Yes, this place is a destination, but it's also a farm, as the large variety of actively-used barns and outbuildings will attest.

There may be better or worse days to visit Terhune Orchards in a relative sense, but there's always something worth checking out: June, when strawberries are beginning to ripen; October, when the fall harvest is in full swing; or the dead of winter, when all that remains of local produce are storage apples and squash. This small farm store reminds you of how fertile New Jersey is and the commanding way the seasons change.

In addition to the store and outbuildings, there's a beautiful, white, colonial farmhouse right next to the parking lot. This is the home of Pam and Gary Mount and their family, the owners of Terhune Orchards since 1975. Even back then, they envisioned the property as a community gathering place and resource. What you see today is the result of that vision.

This is just what they hoped for when they completed a tour of duty in Micronesia with the Peace Corps in the early seventies. Cruising the back roads of Mercer County, they saw a farm with a "For Sale By Owner" sign out front. The sellers, the Terhune family, assumed that a developer would buy it. They never imagined that it would be revived as a farm.

The Terhunes sold them a property, but left them searching for a marketing plan. In those days, retail customers were few and far between; only a handful of shoppers bought at the farm. They also had a stall at the Trenton Farmer's Market, a cooperatively owned mix of farm stands and retail stores in a semi-open wooden building about twenty minutes away. But this wasn't enough. Pam and Gary started the serious job of publicizing. With advertising and mentions in the local press, more people started showing up.

"American Wholesome" is how Pam Mount describes the farm, and for her, it's a place to introduce New Jersey's widely varied population to what the countryside can generate. When it comes to describing how the Mounts choose what they grow, they sound more like artists than business people. "We grow what we like; if it's something we're growing because somebody else likes it, we can't be enthusiastic," is what Pam says. Gary adds, "No matter how much it will sell, if we don't like it, we won't carry it." Judging by the crowds lined up at the farm shop's register, even on a mid-November weekday, this isn't a problem.

Not satisfied with the stream of customers they get from the store, they also sponsor festivals during the year to bring in even more people. The year starts with a "Kite Day" apple blossom festival in the spring and continues with "Apple Days" in the fall that draws so many people they need to hire shuttle buses to help move the crowds around. Finally, in the winter, there's a "Wassailing Party" with chanting, drumming, and traditional English "Molly Dancing."

So really, the best day to visit Terhune Orchards is any day. Whether you are going to pick your own strawberries in the height of summer, buy apples in October and squash in February, or just stop for a cup of coffee and a doughnut on the porch any time, the place is a destination.

# Blueberry-Raspberry Pie

6 TO 8 SERVINGS

You need six cups of berries to make this pie, and for most of the year that many berries are a real luxury. But for those few weeks when the stands are full and there are more berries than you can eat straight, it's time for this recipe.

Preheat the oven to 400°F.

Mix the berries, sugar, nutmeg, and cinnamon together in a large bowl and make sure they are completely blended.

Prepare the bottom crust in a 9-inch pie pan. Pour in the filling and cover it with the top crust. Make a few slits in the top crust for the steam to escape. Bake for 45 minutes or until the fruit bubbles and the crust is golden brown. Let cool at least 10 minutes before serving.

1½ pounds (6 cups) blueberries and/or raspberries in any combination
¾ cup packed brown sugar
1 teaspoon ground nutmeg
1 teaspoon ground cinnamon
1 double batch piecrust dough (see page 193 or 194)

# Mixed Berry Gelatin Mold

4 SERVINGS

With just a tiny bit more effort than opening a box of instant Jell-O, you can make a delicious dessert. This is as much a procedure as it is a recipe. You can substitute all sorts of cut-up fruit (although pineapple will prevent the gelatin from setting) and try different kinds of juices too.

Heat the juice until lukewarm and sprinkle the gelatin over it. Give the mixture a stir every few minutes, until the gelatin is dissolved and there are no blobs, about 10 minutes. Mix in the berries and pour into a 5-cup serving dish. Chill for several hours and serve.

2 cups white grape juice
1 (¼-ounce) packet unflavored gelatin
8 ounces mixed fresh berries (2 cups)

# Fresh Berry Almond Tofu

4 SERVINGS

Almond tofu is a classic Chinese dessert made with soy milk, almond extract, and fruit. However, instead of coagulating it like traditional tofu, this recipe uses gelatin. This keeps it easy, quick, and relatively simple.

Combine the soy milk and syrup in a small pan and heat until it simmers, then remove if from the heat (you may also do this in the microwave). Sprinkle the gelatin over the liquid. Stir gently until the gelatin is dissolved. This may take a few moments. Then add the berries and pour into individual serving dishes. Put them in the refrigerator and chill for several hours. When they're ready to serve, they'll look like white Jell-O.

2 cups soy milk
2 tablespoons almond syrup*
1 (¼-ounce) packet unflavored gelatin
1 pint fresh berries (raspberries and blueberries both work fine)

* The kind used for flavoring espresso drinks works best.

# Sweet and Sour Cantaloupe

4 SERVINGS

This dish does double duty: Served with a fine ham like prosciutto or *jamón serrano*, it makes an flavorful appetizer, but it also makes a great dessert. Give it a try…after all, how many times have you cooked cantaloupe?

With a melon baller, make 3 cups of cantaloupe balls. Combine ¾ cup water, the sugar, vinegar, salt, allspice, cinnamon, and cardamom in a medium pot over low heat and stir until all the sugar and salt dissolve. Bring to a boil and cook for 5 minutes. Add the cantaloupe, and simmer for 5 more minutes, until the melon is just soft. Remove the cantaloupe from the pot and reduce the liquid to a syrup by simmering it for 15 more minutes. Pour over the melon. Let stand for at least 8 hours to deepen the flavor.

1 large cantaloupe
¾ cup sugar
¾ cup white vinegar
1 tablespoon coarse salt
1 whole allspice*
1 cinnamon stick*
4 whole cardamom pods*

* Don't have these spices? You can use 2 teaspoons of pickling spice instead.

# Fox's
# Cranberries

Weekstown, ATLANTIC COUNTY

**182**

On the Garden State Parkway, you'd think suburbia never ends, but get off around exit 50 and you'll see another story entirely: trees, sand, and swamp. Straight, flat roads cut through the forests of the Pine Barrens and are intersected only by wide, lazy rivers and occasional wetlands. Drive for a while, turn left at a tiny sign along a sandy lane, and you'll find a classic south Jersey scene - a swamp, an industrial building, and a farmhouse. This is Fox's Cranberries and that swamp, properly called a "bog," is the farm.

Cranberries are the one major New Jersey crop that's rarely seen fresh at the retail level. Tomatoes, peaches, corn, and eggplants show up at every market, but New Jersey cranberries are often still grown on long-held factory farms and mostly marketed wholesale.

All cranberry bogs began as wild swamp and were cleared and planted in the same way as fields. The grower's cycle of the seasons begins with the onset of winter, when the bogs are flooded with water stored in the farm's reservoir. When the cold sets in, ice forms at the surface and provides a layer of insulation that keeps the berry buds safe. In the spring, the water is pumped out and soon cranberry flowers begin to appear.

During the warmer months, the bog teems with wildlife. Pickerel, frogs, and turtles all make their homes here and large herds of deer come to feed. Traditionally, these bog residents were a major source of food for the people of the Pine Barrens. In fact, they still call venison "Jersey Beef." The Foxes have it on their dinner table frequently.

"We're very fortunate to have such a beautiful property. It's a wonderful place to live. My grandchildren love it here and they cry when they leave," Fox says as she strolls along the causeway that divides her twenty-acre bog in half. What appears to be a lake in the distance is the reservoir that holds the water needed for flooding. It's also twenty acres, the same as the cultivated area. A large diesel pump, about the size of four truck engines, handles the water-moving duties.

Fox's Cranberries has been in the family since 1950, and family legend holds that it was bought under slightly sordid circumstances. Previously, the owners were two partners and the property became available when one murdered the other in an argument. The widow sold it to the Foxes and they replanted. Those very same bushes have been producing ever since.

In the mild climate of southern New Jersey, the berries have a long growing season and the harvest doesn't begin until the middle of October. Cranberries destined for juice and sauce are harvested by the wet method; the bog is flooded and the ripe ones float to the surface where they are picked up by machine. It's very fast, but the fruit is often damaged.

Cranberries that are sold whole, either fresh or frozen, are dry harvested. This is also done by machine, but a much smaller one that looks like a lawn mower with a rakelike mechanism in front. This combs the berries off the bushes and keeps them intact.

Once they're brought back to dry land, they're sorted using a contraption the Foxes call "the bouncer" (officially, it's known as a "Bounce-Board"). This elderly, electrically–powered, wooden device sorts the berries by quality based on a unique principal: The fresher a cranberry is, the higher it will bounce. Rotten, broken, or bruised berries don't bounce at all.

While most of these berries go to a wholesaler for juice and sauce making, Anne takes some to the country living fair in Batsto. There, in a museum village in the heart of the Pine Barrens, a crowd of up to 80,000 will gather and many of them will look for cranberries, the area's number one crop. People are thrilled to buy them from the farmer. Her berries are redder and larger than what's sold in the supermarket and the direct price can't be beat, either for the producer or the consumer.

What does the future hold for Fox's Cranberries? Weekstown is becoming more suburban every year. Teachers, state employees, and other working people move in and force the cost of living up. "To me, a modern farmer is a steward of the land," says Anne Fox. The demand for quality produce will give the region strength and help keep the state more beautiful for everybody.

# Green Tea Cranberry Sauce

YIELDS 2 CUPS

This recipe was inspired by the various fruit tea drinks that are offered everywhere from deli beverage coolers to specialty Asian tea shops. Green tea and five-spice powder add a nice accent to the tartness of the cranberries.

Green Tea Cranberry Sauce can be served anytime a cranberry sauce is called for, as a relish with turkey or roasts.

In a large pot, steep the tea bag in the boiling water for about 4 minutes. Discard the tea bag. Bring the tea back to a simmer and add the sugar and five-spice powder. Stir the mixture; the five-spice powder will take a moment to dissolve. Then add the cranberries and simmer, with occasional stirring, for another 20 minutes, until the cranberries pop and thicken. Serve hot, warm, or cold.

1 green tea bag
2 cups boiling water
¾ cup sugar
1 teaspoon five-spice powder
16 ounces fresh cranberries
  (4 cups)

# Cranberry Cumberland Sauce

YIELDS ABOUT 1½ CUPS

A cranberry sauce with mustard and horseradish? In this recipe, cranberries replace citrus and currants in the classic English condiment, cumberland sauce. This is a great sauce for cold meats. On a buffet, on a sandwich, or with leftovers, cumberland sauce adds a bit of zip.

Put 1 cup water in a medium pot over low heat and add the sugar, stirring until dissolved. Bring to a simmer and stir in the ginger and chiles. Now add the cranberries. You will notice that the heat and stirring will quickly break them down. Sometimes the cranberries will pop as they cook; don't be surprised. Stir in the mustard and horseradish and simmer for about 30 minutes, until it becomes a thick syrup. Remove and discard the pieces of ginger and serve the sauce warm.

½ cup packed brown sugar
3 (¼-inch-thick) slices fresh ginger
2 dried chile peppers, crumbled
12 ounces cranberries (3 cups)
3 tablespoons prepared mustard
2 tablespoons prepared horseradish

# Honey-Rosemary Cranberry Sauce

YIELDS 2 CUPS

This recipe is a twist on the typical cranberries, sugar and gelatin combination that we too often rely on. Serve it warm or at room temperature not only with roasted turkey, but also with Boiled Beef Tongue (page 91).

Combine the apple juice and honey in a soup pot over low heat. Stir to make sure it doesn't burn and the honey is completely dissolved. When the liquid begins to bubble, add the cranberries and rosemary and simmer, uncovered, for 40 minutes stirring frequently. The sauce should thicken to the consistency of pudding. Remember: If you leave it unattended for more than a few moments, it will boil over. Remove the rosemary and let cool.

2 cups apple juice
I cup honey
4 cups fresh cranberries*
I (6-inch) sprig fresh rosemary
  or I tablespoon dried
  rosemary

* Try to use the best—dry-harvested cranberries from a New Jersey producer.

# Tropical Peach Butter

Most on-site farm markets have a corner with large baskets of "utility" fruit. Too ripe to sell as "fancy" or "extra fancy," it's used for cooking, canning or preserving. Here's an easy recipe for that fruit. Peaches are called for here, but it will work fine with almost any fruit that grows in New Jersey. Serve as a dessert topping or as a replacement for jams and jellies.

Combine 2 cups water with the mango juice, sugar, cinnamon, allspice, cloves, cardamom, and lemon juice and bring to a boil. Reduce the heat to a simmer and add the peaches. Continue to cook, uncovered, for 1 hour, stirring occasionally, until the peaches have softened. Remove the cinnamon sticks and run the peach mixture through a food mill or purée it in a food processor. Return the to the pot and simmer on low, stirring occasionally, until the mixture thickens into a jam-like paste—about 2 more hours. Test by spooning a bit onto a plate. If it runs, it still needs a bit more cooking.

2 cups mango juice
½ cup packed brown sugar
2 cinnamon sticks
8 whole allspice
4 whole cloves
4 cardamom pods
1 tablespoon lemon juice
4 pounds peaches, chopped
   (about 12 cups)

# Peaceful Valley Orchards

Peaceful Valley Orchards is truly devoted to quality produce. Its owners, Jeremy and Meredith Compton, grow great fruit and vegetables, sell them in a rustic roadside stand, and bring them to markets in Westfield and Liberty Village.

Meredith and Jeremy came to farming from somewhat different backgrounds. Meredith grew up at the edge of suburbia with horses and acreage, but wanted to have a real working farm. Jeremy was born in New Jersey, but spent much of his childhood on a dairy farm in Wisconsin. That farm was a commercial failure and taught Jeremy some important lessons. But both have a solid agricultural education and share strong knowledge of the market.

The two look so youthful that you'd have a hard time believing that they have as much experience as they do. A thin, cheerful woman with long dark hair, Meredith looks like a graduate student at an agricultural school. In fact, she worked for New Jersey's county extension service for over ten years. With a mop of blond hair shooting out from the edges of his baseball cap, Jeremy looks more ready for mischief than farm work, but he too, had a long career as an agricultural professional before his own full-time farming career began.

Park your car in the lot and Chloe the dog will come running up to you with a corn cob in her mouth. During a visit to Jeremy and Meredith, you might see the animal happily knocking off three or four ears. "Chloe is VERY regular," Meredith laughs.

Vegetarians, both canine and human, will find Peaceful Valley Orchards to be worth a visit. On a main road, not far from I-78, the farm is an easy diversion if you're driving on the highway. And if you just have a few hours to escape the city, you can shoot down 78 to exit 15 and know you'll be at Peaceful Valley within ten minutes of getting off.

Although there's been a Peaceful Valley Orchards in this spot since the 1920s, they've only been selling retail for three years. It started with a roadside canopy tent and as it picked up, they grew along with it. Now, the stand is an old, converted barn, with good lighting, a cooler stocked with free-range eggs, and shelves and bins filled with all that Peaceful Valley produce.

"The demand is for the big three: tomatoes, peaches, and corn. For some reason, people can identify with Jersey tomatoes, there's nothing like them," Jeremy reports. And Peaceful Valley grows a lot of tomatoes: heirlooms, pear tomatoes, and just plain big, red, slicing tomatoes. Peaches are the next of the "big three," and they offer both yellow and white varieties. Corn is just as important, and what the dog doesn't eat, customers take from the big piles on display, examining each ear as if it were a sculpture being appraised.

Eating Peaceful Valley's eggplants, apples, pears, and squashes, you can see that they are every bit as excellent as the "big three," even if they're not quite as appealing in the markets. But for the Comptons, the "big three" rule their tastes too. "Our favorite food here on the farm is tomatoes. We don't eat tomatoes all year until ours are ready and it's the same with sweet corn."

Meredith is one of the few people who's willing to violate the "only eat heirloom tomatoes raw" rule. She cans them and even makes sauce out of them and encourages consumers to do the same. She also makes her own applesauce and a custom-blended apple-pear sauce. Nothing grown on the farm goes to waste.

People have a way of finding Peaceful Valley. They stop at the stand, see them at farmer's markets, and find them on the Internet (www.peacefulvalleyorchards.com). "We're not into entertainment farming. We don't have corn mazes or hay rides or haunted houses," notes Jeremy, but a trip to Peaceful Valley will still offer great rewards: baskets of peaches, eggplants, apples, and pears. Those strange looking heirloom tomatoes that are each uniquely perfect in their own way, and onions and potatoes—those poor unsung heroes of the farm stand—are all there.

Jeremy says that the stand is the best way to reach buyers: "It's more personable here. We get return customers. At Westfield, you don't have time to chit-chat, but here, people bring us Christmas gifts, and even bring the dog gifts." The Comptons treasure this bond with their clientele. He continues, "You start throwing your product on the wholesale, worldwide market and you're done." And with that, he goes off to the stand to greet a few more shoppers. Before he walks away, he shares one of his greatest secrets: The dog may love corn, but Jeremy's favorite food is steak!

Don't tell anybody.

# Five-Spice Stewed Peaches

4 SERVINGS

You'll encounter the distinctive five-spice flavor in all sorts of Chinese meat, sweet and savory dishes. (See Chinese-Style Tea Eggs, page 68). The spice also works well with fruit. Serve it as a dessert with ice cream for an interesting end to a meal.

In a large saucepan, melt the butter over low heat and add the five-spice powder. Then brown the peaches in this mixture for a few moments. Add the sugar and 1½ cups water to the pan and bring to a boil. Lower to a simmer and cook for 10 minutes, until the peaches are tender. Remove the peaches and reserve. Reduce the remaining liquid to a syrup by cooking it over low heat for another 15 minutes or so. (Be careful here; keep stirring, it burns easily!) Pour over the cooked peaches.

1 tablespoon butter
1 teaspoon five-spice powder
4 peaches, pitted and sliced
1 cup packed brown sugar

# Peach Custard

8 SERVINGS

A classic dessert that captures the flavor of fresh peaches. Don't be afraid of the bain-marie! It's just a fancy French term for a pan of water, and it helps to cook the custard evenly.

Preheat the oven to 375°F and grease 8 (4-ounce) ramekins.

**2 pounds yellow peaches, pitted and chopped**
**1½ cups sugar**
**¼ cup amaretto liqueur**
**5 eggs, lightly beaten**
**1 cup milk**

Put the peaches and sugar in a large pot and cook over medium heat until the peaches disintegrate. (Cooking time depends on the ripeness of the peaches but should be about 45 minutes.) Let them cool down and then purée with the amaretto, eggs, and milk in a food processor. Pour the mixture into the prepared ramekins so they are about two-thirds full and place them in a bain-marie. (Take a baking dish and put about ½ inch of water in it. The water shouldn't be high enough to splash into the custard.) Put the whole thing in the oven for 40 minutes, until the top begins to brown and a toothpick inserted in the middle comes out dry. Cool and serve.

# Slow-Baked Fruit

4 SERVINGS

If you've got the oven on all day with a slow-roasted meat dish, you might want to add a pan of fruit for a dessert. You can have both going at the same time and be even more ready at meal-time.

Preheat the oven to 225°F. Spread the fruit out on a non-stick baking sheet. Sprinkle the sugar evenly over it. Bake for 2 hours, until the fruit is soft and caramelized. Serve warm.

2 apples, cored and quartered
2 pears, cored and quartered
2 tablespoons packed brown sugar

# Piecrust with Butter and Lard

I DOUBLE BATCH PIECRUST

Even if you're careful about what you eat ninety-nine percent of the time, there are moments when you're going to have to have something more. When that happens, it's time for pie made with a lard crust. Is lard less healthy than butter or shortening? That's a question for researchers. But the combination of butter and lard makes a pastry that's both tender and flaky.

Put the flour and salt in a large bowl. Add the lard and start working it into the flour with a pastry cutter (or your fingertips). After a few moments, the mixture will resemble corn kernels. Sprinkle the dough with the vinegar and keep going. When the vinegar is mixed in, add the butter and continue blending for about 3 more minutes. Add water, a few drops at a time, until you're able to form the dough into a ball. When this happens, cover it with plastic wrap, and refrigerate for at least 30 minutes.

2 cups all-purpose flour
1 teaspoon salt
½ cup chilled lard, cut into small
 pieces
2 tablespoons cider vinegar
¼ cup chilled unsalted butter,
 cut into small pieces
Ice water

Now it's time to **ROLL THE CRUST OUT:** Cut the dough in half, sprinkle some flour on a board and use a rolling pin to flatten the dough into a ⅛ inch thin sheet. It's now ready to use. Repeat with the second half or wrap well and refrigerate for a future use.

# Whole Wheat Piecrust

1 DOUBLE BATCH PIECRUST

There are dozens of piecrust recipes out there and all of them have something in them that will scare somebody. This recipe is for those who can't eat pork or saturated fat, or who need a whole grain alternative. It has no lard and uses whole wheat flour. Even vegans can eat this. Be aware that baking times will be substantially longer than with white flour and saturated fat crusts.

Sift the flour, salt, and sugar together in a large bowl and then add the oil, water, and vinegar. Use your fingers—don't be afraid, just dive right in!—and blend the mixture into a dough. Mold the dough into a ball, cover it with plastic wrap, and chill for an hour or so. Roll out to a thickness of about ⅛ inch.

3 cups whole wheat flour
1 teaspoon salt
1 teaspoon packed brown sugar
1 cup vegetable oil
½ cup ice water
3 tablespoons cider vinegar

**VARIATIONS:** With savory pies like a chicken pot pie (page 58), omit the sugar and substitute 2 teaspoons garlic salt for the regular salt.

**NOTE:** Don't be ashamed to substitute a premade crust if you want to get something in the oven quickly.

# INGREDIENT GLOSSARY

In a state as diverse as New Jersey, it's impossible for any one person to be familiar with a complete cross section of the foods eaten here. This is a list of foods used in this book that need a bit more comment or explanation than can be included in a typical recipe.

It's also worth noting that as a general rule, imported items are far cheaper in ethnic markets than in supermarkets and that farmer's markets not only have lower prices, but also higher quality than almost any other venue.

**ALMOND SYRUP**——The almond flavoring used at espresso bars is almost always imported from Italy. It's a simple sugar base infused with almond flavoring. It can often be found in the coffee section of the supermarket. Look for products that use natural almond flavor instead of an artificial substitute.

**AMARETTO**—An Italian liqueur that can be purchased in small bottles at almost any liquor store. Used here as a flavoring for desserts.

**ANCHO CHILE**——A spicy chile with smoky undertones. It is available whole or ground in the Mexican sections of supermarkets in Latino groceries.

**ANCHOVIES**—Canned anchovies are sold two ways: either packed in oil or salt. Oil-packed anchovies are ready to use straight from the can, but the ones packed in salt have a more delicate flavor. These require careful filleting. In this book, some recipes use them as part of the flavor base and others, like *Bagna Cauda* (page 97) use them as a main ingredient. Give them a try before rejecting them out of hand! And buy them in large quantities; they are much cheaper and they last forever.

**ARTICHOKE HEARTS**——Fresh artichokes are tough to clean and hard to come by out of season, but frozen ones are always available in most supermarkets. The recipe in this book will not work with the canned or jar-packed varieties, which are often pre-seasoned.

**ASIAN PEARS**——Similar to western pears in shape and color, but not flavor.

**BACON**—Simply Grazin' Farm (page 76) offers great bacon. Otherwise, Pennsylvania Dutch markets and local butchers are the places to go. Try to avoid mass-market products that have lots of salt but little flavor.

**BAKING POWDER**—The common double-acting variety is clearly marked as such on the label. Don't use a package that's been open more than a year or so. It loses strength after opening.

**BASIL**—Well-Sweep Herb Farm (page 124) sells more fresh varieties on-site than you ever imagined existed. It's used fresh in sauces and salads. Many of the others will have one or two types for sale. In the off season, make do with what's available in better supermarkets or specialty stores, but it's a real treat right from the farm.

**BAY LEAF**—A leaf used for seasoning stews, curries and other dishes. Best bought in Indian groceries or stores with bulk spice sections.

**BISON** (all cuts)—Also known as the "American Buffalo." They're similar to beef, but with slightly stronger flavor. Sometimes available from butchers or supermarkets, but a trip to the Readington River Buffalo Company (page 86) is well worth it for the experience.

**BLACK BEAN GARLIC SAUCE/PASTE**—Comes in small jars and can be found in the Asian sections of supermarkets or at a far lower prices at Chinese grocery stores. Keep it covered and in the refrigerator and it will last for 2 to 3 months.

**BUFFALO**—properly known as the "American Bison," they should not be confused with the Italian "buffala"—known in English as the "Water Buffalo."

**BROTH, CHICKEN/BEEF/FISH/VEGETABLE**—The soup section of most supermarkets has them in one-quart containers. These have a far better flavor than instants or concentrates.

**BULLION CUBES**—even of the same brand—vary widely. Those made for the Chinese, Japanese, and Korean markets seem to have far better flavor. Pick them up when you visit one of New Jersey's great Asian superstores.

**CALAMARI/SQUID**—These words are used interchangeably. Buy frozen and cleaned in ring form unless you are certain they are fresh. Do NOT trust unknown fish stores for this information.

**CARAWAY SEEDS**—Used as a topping and garnish, they are best bought from bulk spice suppliers.

**CARDAMOM PODS**—Used as a seasoning. Both black and green varieties can be found in any Indian grocery.

**CELERY ROOT/CELERIAC**——That strange looking root you've seen in the produce aisle but never bothered to try. Think of it as a cross between the taste of celery and the texture of a potato.

**CHILES PEPPERS, CRUSHED/FLAKES**—Also called "red pepper flakes." Look for this product in the Latino section of supermarkets. It's also available (at a much lower price of course) at ethnic markets.

**CHILE PEPPERS, DRIED**—Available in the Latino sections of supermarkets at lower prices. Also can be bought at Chinese and Indian stores. When dried isn't specified, recipes here call for fresh.

**CHILE PEPPER OIL**—Sold in most Asian markets and can sometimes be found in the Asian section of good supermarkets, sometimes marketed as hot pepper oil.

**CHIPOTLE PEPPERS**——Smoked jalapeño chiles packed in adobo sauce. Very hot, with a complex, smoky flavor, they're sold in small cans in the Mexican section of most supermarkets. You can also find them dried. Rehydrate dried chipotles in warm water and use as for the canned type.

**CHORIZO**—A spicy, dry pork sausage. Small ones are often available in the supermarket, but a visit to a Latino grocery will get you better quality, choice, and price. If you are lucky enough to see fresh ones behind a meat counter somewhere, snatch them right up!

**COCONUT MILK**——Canned coconut milk seems to be available everywhere these days but is cheapest in the big Chinese or Indian stores. It has many uses in Asian cooking but in these recipes, it's for curries and desserts. Imported, frozen coconut has a better flavor and can sometimes be found at the same sources.

**CRANBERRIES**—Look for "dry-harvested" local berries. A visit to the Pine Barrens during harvest time will be well rewarded. You can learn everything you ever wanted to know about cranberries and then some by attending the Chatsworth Cranberry Festival in late October. Be sure to look for Anne Fox from Fox's Cranberries (page 182).

**CURRY PASTE, VINDALOO/GARAM MASALA/MILD**—— Comes in 10-ounce jars that should be refrigerated after opening. Far cheaper in Indian groceries than in supermarkets.

**CURRY PASTE, THAI GREEN OR RED**——Can be found in plastic tubs or small jars at most Chinese groceries or in small cans in some supermarkets. Thai grocery stores seem to pop up around the state and then vanish. If you know of one, it's worth a visit for this and whole host of other products.

**CILANTRO, DRIED**—Similar in flavor to the fresh leaves, the dried product holds up better in long-cooked dishes. Available in the Latino sections of supermarkets. Also known as fresh coriander.

**CORIANDER, GROUND**—The ground seed of the coriander plant. The leaves and stems are more frequently called "cilantro in New Jersey stores." Available in the Latino sections of supermarkets at lower prices.

**FISH SAUCE/THAI FISH SAUCE**—Different names for the same product, fermented sauces used for seasoning Asian dishes. Other kinds, like Philippine fish sauce, will be marked as such. Buy at a good Chinese market or at a local supermarket for a much higher price.

**FIVE-SPICE POWDER**—A classic Chinese combination of cinnamon, cloves, fennel seed, star anise, and Szechuan peppercorns that can be bought from most Chinese groceries. Traditionally, it's used for braising and stews, but in this book, we also cook fruit with it.

**GARLIC SALT**—Varies greatly in quality. The best, with a strong garlic flavor and no chemical aftertaste, seems to be sold in Brazilian and Portuguese stores and needs to be refrigerated after opening. Look for the Portuguese words *alho e sal*, "garlic and salt."

**GINGER**—The root has a pungent and somewhat spicy flavor that works well in sautéed and braised dishes. With sweetening, it also finds its way into sweets and drinks. (ginger snaps, ginger ale) Always means fresh ginger in this book. It's sold in most supermarkets and just about any Asian store. Usually you peel off its thin skin before cooking, using the edge of a spoon or knife.

**ITALIAN SEASONING**—A combination of spices, such as oregano, basil, marjoram, rosemary and sage, sold in most stores. Of course, it's much cheaper at bulk spice outlets. Here's a typical recipe:

2 tablespoons dried oregano
2 tablespoons dried basil
1 tablespoon dried marjoram
½ tablespoon dried rosemary
1 tablespoon dried sage

Mix the oregano, basil, marjoram, rosemary, and sage together in a dry container with a tightly closeable lid. Use as called for in recipes, in stews, with sautéed vegetables, or on pizzas.

**JAPANESE SEASONING/FURIKAKE**—A packaged condiment made in Japan and sold in shaker jars. You can buy it at most Asian superstores or in the Asian sections of supermarkets.

**KIMCHEE**—Korean pickled vegetables with a deeply spicy and sour flavor. Can be bought at most Asian markets. Often absurdly overpriced at supermarkets.

**L I M O N C E L L O**—A sweet, and lemon flavored liqueur from southern Italy available at good liquor stores.

**M A N G O   J U I C E**—Try to find a product without too much added sugar. Indian groceries are your best bet.

**M U S T A R D   P O W D E R**—Ground mustard seeds, which also make what most of us call prepared mustard. Buy from a bulk spice or Chinese market.

**N U T M E G**—Available at any Indian grocery for a tiny fraction of the price anywhere else. It's sold in two forms. Ground nutmeg for making dried spice blends or whole nutmeg that you grind yourself. Try to use the whole form when you can.

**O R E G A N O ,   D R I E D**—Well-stocked spice shops sell it in two forms; Mexican and Mediterranean (or Italian). Try to use the form that's appropriate to the origin of the dish you're cooking, but if you want to keep just one in your pantry, the Mediterranean variety will do just fine.

**O Y S T E R S**—Make sure you buy them live and in the shell if you're eating them raw, but the shucked ones can be substituted for cooked dishes. As is so often the case, they are cheaper at Asian markets.

**P A L M   S U G A R**—Used in Thai and Indian dishes and sold in Indian markets. If it's the only ingredient you're missing, substitute raw or demerara sugar.

**P A R M E S A N   C H E E S E**—A hard cheese from the Parma region of Italy that is often grated and used as a seasoning. If you buy it grated, make sure it still has some moisture and isn't the consistency of dust. If you see stale, dried out rinds or blocks of the stuff for sale at a reasonable price, buy them and treat them like bones—freeze them and add them to soups for a vivid cheese flavor. Don't try to grind them into a seasoning, you'll just get a stale taste.

**P A R S L E Y**—An herb used for flavor in many cuisines. Markets offer two types "regular" parsley has a coarse texture and a slightly bitter flavor that works well in Middle Eastern dishes. Italian parsley is a milder and leafier. Parsley is also used as a garnish. Don't be afraid to substitute one for the other as long as you don't accidentally use cilantro, which is sometimes called "Chinese Parsley."

**P O P P Y   S E E D S**—Are a seasoning and garnish often seen in eastern European cooking. They are cheapest bought from bulk spice suppliers.

**R E D   P E P P E R ,   G R O U N D / C A Y E N N E ,   P A P R I K A** — Ground red peppers are used as a seasoning in almost every corner of the world. Cayenne are a specific type of red pepper, as is paprika. The heat and flavor can vary widely, even among packages of the same brand. Available at any Indian grocery for a tiny fraction of the price anywhere else.

**RICE, RISOTTO/BASMATI**—Try to buy good-quality rice in the largest quantity you have space for. Naturally, rice is far cheaper in ethnic markets than it is in the supermarket. Look for basmati in Indian shops and risotto in Italian markets.

**SAGE**—Farm stands with good herb sections will have sage. Otherwise, get it fresh from the herb section of your supermarket. If you want to grow your own, get sage plants from Well-Sweep Herb Farm (page 124).

**SALT**—Try sea salt, it has a flavor that is free of chemical and bitter overtones. Portuguese shops sell this for a fraction of the price of supermarkets, Italian gourmet stores, or health food stores.

**SESAME SEEDS**——Come in colors ranging from white to black with pale gold being most typical. Legend has it that the darker they are, the more flavor they have, but many are just dyed black to command a higher price.

**SHERRY**—A fortified wine sometimes labeled "dry" or "cream." Use one fit for drinking rather than the strange, salted cooking sherries sold for cooking. Think of sherry as adding an intense, wine-like flavor.

**SOFRITO**——A thick seasoning paste of vegetables, fat, and annatto seeds, sold in Latino markets or the Latino sections of supermarkets. It's used as a base and flavoring in soups, stews and braised dishes.

**SOY SAUCE**—The soy sauce sold in Chinese markets will taste better and be much cheaper than what's in the supermarket. Look for brands that are actually brewed from soybeans rather than produced by an industrial process. But beware; there are still great variations in flavor. Try a few brands and see what you like.

**SUMAC, GROUND**—Wild berries dried, ground into a powder and available in Middle Eastern and Turkish stores. It gives a tangy and unique flavor; don't leave it out!

**TAMARIND PASTE**—A sticky, sweet-sour pulp from the tamarind tree that can be bought from most Asian groceries.

**TRIPE**—Beef, or sheep stomach linings often used in French, Italian, Asian or Latino cooking. Try to get it from producers, but ethnic grocers will carry it too.

**VINEGAR**— Many dishes call for specific vinegars and are an important flavor component. Chinese rice wine, Japanese mirin, and Spanish sherry vinegar are examples of this. Most types of vinegar are easily found in the supermarket, but white wine vinegar is far cheaper in Portuguese stores.

**WALNUT OIL** —Pressed from walnuts, it has a deep nutty flavor that compliments many salads, pastas and other dishes. You can find this at the local supermarket in the oil section. Be aware, that once opened, it only lasts a few months.

**YAM LEAVES** —A traditional Chinese green available from Chia-Sin Farm (page 156) and the better Chinese markets. Yam leaves are a bit more bitter and deeply flavored than spinach. They're in the same family, but not from the same plant that produces the root vegetable called "yams."

# A STATE of SECRET TREASURES

## THE NEW JERSEY FOOD SHOPPING GUIDE

New Jersey's wonderful combination of vibrant farmer's markets and thriving ethnic communities makes it one of the best places in the country to buy food, but when it's three o'clock on a Saturday afternoon and you're stuck in a traffic jam on Route 1, the fact that almost any edible known to mankind can be had somewhere in the state won't be of much comfort to you. Some of the ingredients called for in this book are as simple as a chicken or a carrot and some others are a bit harder to find. Even so, with a bit of planning, you can make food shopping an adventure and find that many farms, shops, and markets are worthy destinations.

Often, the biggest problem with serious food shopping is simply the lack of knowledge about a given area. In many places, everybody knows where all the neighborhoods are. Any New Yorker can find Little Italy, but few long-time New Jersey residents could locate its thriving Indian, Korean, and Portuguese neighborhoods, even though in each case, they are the largest of their kind in the eastern United States.

With this in mind, here's a guide to some of the best sources for many of the ingredients listed in this book. Remember, farm visits may take you to the rural fringes of this very crowded state, but these stores will bring you right into the urban core. Of course, this is only a small percentage of what's out there. If you see something else interesting along the way, don't hesitate to give it a try.

### THE UNION SQUARE GREENMARKET

You might think that the best of New Jersey's farm produce appears at roadside stands along idyllic country lanes. You may also imagine elegant shops in upscale suburban communities, but the place to find New Jersey's best farm goods isn't even in New Jersey—it's in New York City's Greenmarkets.

The Council On the Environment of New York City runs these markets at over forty locations in all five boroughs. But the one food fans are most likely to be familiar with is at Union Square in lower Manhattan. This is the one you're likely to see when famous chefs are shown going to market on TV or in slick food magazines. As one knowledgeable person put it, Union Square is "the Harvard and the Hollywood" of farmer's markets.

On Mondays, Wednesdays, Fridays, and Saturdays, farmers from as far as 200 miles away put their best foot forward for a chance to sell to this well-heeled, and very particular crowd.

Walking through the Union Square market, there is no sign of Harvard and only a small touch of Hollywood, but there is no question that this is the big time. The crowds are larger, the displays are bigger, and there are a greater number of vendors than in the other greenmarkets. These aren't just a few farmers who shot down the Turnpike; instead, stands appear from farms in every direction. Some are as close as Stokes Farm (page 141) and others as far away as the Finger Lakes of upstate New York.

Shoppers really look like city people. Men in suits, women in high heels, and everybody wearing the most knowledgeable look imaginable. There isn't a child to be seen and the dogs are as well groomed as their chic owners.

All in all though, this is still a farmer's market. What's there is still what the land has to offer. There's nothing that's been flown in or gassed or waxed or dyed. It's the honest harvest of the vendors.

Located at the corner of 17th Street and Broadway in Manhattan.
www.cenyc.org/HTMLGM/maingm.htm
8:00 A.M. to 6:00 P.M. Mondays, Wednesdays, Fridays, and Saturdays. Year-round.

## JERSEY FRESH:
## NEW JERSEY COMMUNITY FARMER'S MARKETS

Every weekend during growing season, and on many weekdays too, farmers from all over New Jersey bring their produce to sell at farmer's markets. From Lafayette in the north to Salem in the south, there are vegetables, fruit, eggs, poultry, meat and the occasional piece of cheese.

These markets aren't exclusively for farmers – bakers, kids doing fund raising, shepherds selling wool, and a whole host of other community activities often go on here—but it's all part of the show. This is where you'll get to meet the growers and buy at reasonable prices. Vendors work hard to create impressive displays and sometimes there's almost a race to see if they can put the food out faster than local consumers can buy it.

Few of these markets have permanent locations and state and local officials are always trying to get more sellers, so it's hard to give addresses from one year to the next. Look for big "Jersey Fresh" banners for the details. And of course, you can find details on the Internet: www.state.nj.us/jerseyfresh/searches/urban.htm will give you a complete and up-to-date listing.

## CORRADO'S FAMILY AFFAIR

Corrado's isn't the place to shop if all you need is a quarter of a pound of cheese or a single pack of pasta; the store is huge and the lines are long. Nor is Corrado's the place to go for elegant gourmet items. Many other stores in New Jersey can provide wonderful luxuries but Corrado's is the place to go for quality basics, especially in large quantities.

Grab a cart when you enter! You'll need it for the great buys on things like canned tomatoes, jars of pesto, and bulk spices. Look carefully and you'll find 28-ounce cans of anchovies for about ten bucks—they're almost two dollars an ounce at most supermarkets. It's the same with cold cuts, prepared salads, and cheeses—buy in bulk and save a bundle. Add the widest range of dried pasta you'll see anywhere.

In addition to this huge selection of food, there is an extensive Italian-oriented housewares section. This is the place to find all those items that Italians take for granted, but just aren't fancy enough to make it to more elegant shops—a one-cup espresso pot here, doesn't mean one the size of an American mug; instead there's a tiny pot that makes what we would call a single "shot" of coffee.

Across from the food store is a garden center, a shop with beer brewing and winemaking supplies, and last but not least, a "wholesale food warehouse" where you can find even bigger versions of the items they carry.

1578 Main Avenue
Clifton, NJ 07011
800-232-6758; 973-340-0628
www.corradosmarket.com
5:00 A.M. to 9:00 P.M. Monday through Wednesday, and Saturday
5:00 A.M. to 10:00 P.M. Thursday and Friday
5:00 A.M. to 8:00 P.M. Sunday

## HAN AH REUM KOREAN SUPERMARKET

When people in the New York area talk about "Korean markets," they really mean two different things. First, a sort of produce and convenience store run by Korean immigrants and second, a store that sells Korean foods and other items. The very large Korean immigrant population in New Jersey guarantees plenty of stores in the second category, but none are even half as complete as Han Ah Reum.

Han Ah Reum is a mall anchored by a large supermarket in the heart of a particularly bleak section of Routes 1 and 9 (called Broad Avenue here), just south of the George Washington Bridge. This is the sort of neighborhood that confirms skeptic's worst nightmares about New Jersey.

Sleazy looking motels, endless rows of warehouses, no-brand gas stations, and occasional construction sites are what you see here. A suspicious person could spend lots of time wondering about who is staying in those motels.

This isn't a place you can run into for a few items! Expect to spending a couple of hours here if you're even the least bit curious about any aspect of Korean culture. Besides the supermarket, there are specialty shops for fashion, gifts, ginseng, books, videos, and music. Another remarkable store sells supplies for Korean paper crafts

The liquor store is a lesson in the Korean art of gift-giving. Single malt scotches, brandies, cognacs, and even ouzo are available. Just browsing the shelves makes you imagine businessmen in suits handing each other gift-wrapped boxes of this stuff. A dusty corner holds wine and beer for home consumption.

The Japanese-style coffee house gives you the feeling of being in the Tokyo subway system even if you've never been out of New Jersey. In fact, a few minutes sipping a cup of coffee will prove the theory that you don't ever have to leave the state because everything in the world eventually comes here.

In the supermarket, the produce section really has a Korean slant with at least a dozen typical vegetables. The onions and garlic are beautiful and there is a wide variety of cabbages and other greens. Fish on ice is also far better than usual. Monkfish, beltfish, red snapper, skate wing and a host of others are fresh and well displayed. Of course, there is aisle after aisle of Korean groceries. Soup stocks, teas, chili pastes, seaweed, and noodles fill the shelves. Fiber fanatics will find brown rice cakes, a welcome addition to the list of unrefined rice products available here. Of course, Lotte Choco Pies, the junk food of choice for generations of Koreans, were on sale the day I first visited.

The appliance section is so interesting that it could be the basis for a PhD dissertation in something like "Kitchen Anthropology." Large electric kimchee fermenters, rice cake makers, Hello Kitty rice cookers, and tiny washers and dryers are all on display.
Within a two-minute walk, are several Korean restaurants and beauty parlors. You really have the feeling of being in the center of the Korean universe.

321 Broad Avenue
Ridgefield, NJ 07657
201-943-9600
www.hanahreum.com
8:00 A.M. to 11:00 P.M. 7 days a week

# HONG KONG SUPERMARKET

No Asian ingredient would have the audacity to not show up at the amazingly complete Hong Kong Supermarkets. Whatever you need, think you might need, or had no idea you needed is here, and in astounding variety.

Both Hong Kong Supermarkets are large suburban supermarkets devoted to Asian food and no stone is left unturned. You'll find the region's biggest selection of everything from *sushi nori* to canned tropical fruit.

Fish? Fresh, frozen, or dried?

Duck? With or without the head?

The Hong Kong Supermarkets give you a real sense of just how huge the world of Asian pasta is—I dare you to count the varieties! You can also find a dozen types of bouillon cubes in Asian flavors that include my own favorite, "Chinese Ham," as well as "seafood" and "wonton." Here, the indecisive can spend ages choosing a soy sauce from the several dozen available varieties. The aisle of frozen dumplings has kept my wife Maria busy for hours.

If you do take hours, don't worry! Each store has a food court with great Chinese meals and snacks. There are noodle soups, three-dish lunch specials, and a host of other things worth eating, all at rock bottom prices. The East Brunswick store has a nice little sushi bar too.

3600 Park Avenue at Oak Tree Road
South Plainfield, NJ 07080
908-668-8862
9:30 A.M. to 8:30 P.M. 7 days a week

265 State Route 18
East Brunswick, NJ, 08816
732-651-8288
9:30 A.M. to 8:30 P.M. 7 days a week

## NOURI'S BROTHERS SHOPPING CENTER

Have you ever tasted fresh pita bread? Did you ever think that it could exist in any form but those plastic bags you find in supermarkets and delis? At Nouri's Brothers, the biggest Middle Eastern store in New Jersey, you can try pitas in at least a half dozen different forms; large, small, whole wheat, herbed and more, all straight from the oven.

Nouri's Brothers isn't just for fresh bread though. It's the first place to look for all sorts of products from the Middle East. It's filled with unusual spices—this is where you can find ground sumac for Kofta Kebobs (page 79). There are also regional cheeses and condiments as well as a great variety of Middle Eastern versions of Mediterranean favorites. The most notable of these are olives and olive oil. Lebanese extra virgin is excellent and about one third the price of a similar Italian product.

While you're visiting Nouri's, don't forget to check out the rest of the neighborhood. It is a miniature trip to the Middle East. This is urban immigrant culture at its most vivid. Stop at a café for pastries and coffee, enjoy a full meal at a white tablecloth Turkish restaurant, and soak up the atmosphere. Of course, if you stroll a couple of blocks too far, you'll wind up at Corrado's (page 205), with its great selection of cold cuts, bulk seasonings, pastas, and a great little Italian hardware selection. Only in New Jersey!

997–1001 Main Street
Patterson, NJ 07503
800-356-6874 (800 EL NOURI)
8:00 A.M. to 8:00 P.M. 7 days a week

## PA DUTCH FARM MARKET

This is a sort of Amish market within a strip mall a couple of miles north of Princeton on Route 27. First of all, ignore the promising looking, but truly awful, snack bar and the sad, strange produce stand; instead, go for the meats and pickles.

The two outstanding meat counters, Beiler's Fresh Meats and Stoltzfus Fresh Poultry make the PA Dutch Farm Market worth the drive from almost anywhere in New Jersey. Beiler's is the sort of great butcher you dream about on those days when the supermarket fails you. There are cold cuts, traditional sausages (don't look for turkey, pesto, or kiwi as a sausage flavor here!), and very high-quality beef, pork, lamb, and veal.

Stoltzfus Fresh Poultry sells some of the best birds I've ever eaten. Drug- and hormone-free chickens and turkeys are available both whole and butchered. The turkey London broil is a favorite of mine. This is one of the few turkey cuts I've eaten that can take the place of chicken in many recipes.

Also at Pennsylvania Dutch Farm Market is Lapp's Salads, which sells great pickles straight from the barrel, as well as many brands of preserved foods from Lancaster County, Pennsylvania. Look for Kaufman's fruit butters and spreads, local honey, and interesting deli salads.

Kingston Mall, Route 27
Kingston, NJ 08528
9:30 A.M. to 6:00 P.M. Thursday
9:00 A.M. to 7:00 P.M. Friday
9:00 A.M. to 4:00 P.M. Saturday

## SPIKE'S FISH MARKET

415 Broadway at Channel Drive
Point Pleasant Beach, NJ 08742
732-295-9400
10:00 A.M. to 10:00 P.M. 7 days a week

## CO-OP SEAFOOD

57 Channel Drive
Point Pleasant Beach, NJ08742
732-899-2211
9:00 A.M. to 9:00 P.M. 7 days a week

If you try to visit the beach resort of Point Pleasant on a hot summer day, you might not think it is all that pleasant. Rows of motels, snack bars, and convenience stores line the few traffic-clogged roads that lead to the beach, and if you want something other than pizza, hot dogs, or Italian ices to eat, you might think you're out of luck, but all you have to do is drive down the town's one back street and you'll strike gold.

Channel Drive runs behind the motels and along the inlet. Instead of more motels, it is home to a small and vibrant commercial fishing industry and it is here that you'll find two of the rarest of New Jersey rarities: good fish stores. Both Spike's and Co-op are of the same format—combination fish market/restaurants—and both will have at least a couple of different kinds of fish fresh off those same fishing boats you see tied up outside.

On the day I visited, there was local hake (not just fillets; they had a whole fish, the first time I'd ever seen it), flounder, tuna, and clams, as well as a few standards like salmon and shrimp. All had reasonable, but not bargain, prices.

When the sun is shining and the beach is crowded, both of these places are jam-packed with people eating fish and chips, broiled fish plates, seafood salads, and raw bar items. In fact, Spike's has a nice little dining room with basic service. I had their Shrimp Parmigiano hero, a sandwich that could be a lesson in sauce for most other New Jersey sandwich shops. Co-op is a bit more simple. You order at the counter and can either eat inside at the tables lined up by the raw fish display cases or on picnic tables outside. You will be happy in either case.

## PORFIRIO'S ITALIAN FOOD

If you were asked to create the perfect Italian-American store for a Hollywood movie, you would put it on a tree-lined block in an obviously working class neighborhood with clean streets and well-kept row houses. Then you would staff it with a great-looking gray-haired guy with a thick southern Italian accent and add a few oddball characters—perhaps a guy with a buzz cut and tattoos delivering cases of canned anchovies.

The back room would have its own scene—a couple of country girls (from the Italian countryside of course!) in white aprons and chef's hats making gnocchi from scratch, peeling potatoes, breaking eggs, and doing the sorts of things that most of us believe only Italian country girls can do.

Your store wouldn't stock anything favored by Martha Stewart types but would never run out of anything needed to make basic Italian foods. Good strong olive oil, anchovies with chile peppers, fresh mozzarella and ricotta, and just a few really fine hams and salamis.

Of course, you would never have to go to the trouble to create such a store because it already exists—Porfirio's Italian Food in the Chambersburg section of Trenton, New Jersey.

Chambersburg is a surprising place, a well-kept, unrestored neighborhood in an otherwise crumbling city. Food is the area's main claim to fame. The street signs feature table settings, and old-style Italian restaurants dot the streets. If you spend some time strolling, you may find yourself imagining life in one of these great old row-houses. In this dream life, all your problems vanish and your home cooking is always simple, Italian, and wonderful.

Go to Porfirio's, go to shop in the only store in New Jersey that sells truffles without the slightest bit of pretense, go and watch the pretty girls in the back make pasta, go and have the boss draw you a shot of espresso from the little machine behind the counter.

320 Anderson Street
Trenton, NJ 08611
609-393-4116
8:30 A.M. to 6:00 P.M. Tuesday through Friday
8:30 A.M. to 5:00 P.M. Saturdays
8:30 A.M. to 2:00 P.M. Sundays
Fresh ravioli on Sundays only

## A.J. SEABRAS SUPERMARKETS

At other places, the bread may be a throwback to what European immigrants ate 100 years ago, or it might be an attempt to outdo the finest bakers in Paris or Milan, but only in Seabras is it a perfect recreation of what typical Latin Europeans eat today.

What makes this place worth the trip? Portuguese and Brazilian food products, many of which can't be found anyplace else, at rock bottom prices. Canned tuna in extra virgin olive oil as good as the best from the Amalfi coast, on special one week for $1.59. That bread is also a bargain. Those rolls that look exactly like the bread you see in Spain or Italy (but taste even better) are less than fifty cents each.

Fish stands out here: particularly, the fresh sardines, but also the amazing salt cod department—it really is a whole department, not just a few plastic-wrapped pieces.

The meat department? is fairly typical for an urban Hispanic neighborhood, with bright colors, low prices, and an amazing selection of different kinds of lard. You really don't know how many different kinds of fat a pig's body contains until you see what's available here. There is also a good variety of sausages. You'll find chorizo, the Spanish kind not the Mexican one, and blood sausages. Of course, there are all the meats for making feijoada, the Brazilian national dish.

Seabras also offer a few surprises: olives and olive oil are a bargain here and fine sherry vinegar—a delicious and less sweet alternative to Italian balsamic—is well worth buying. Another good find is Portuguese ham, a nice cross between Italian prosciutto and American country ham available whole, thinly sliced, or in chunks. Cheese is also worth shopping for here. They have a wide assortment of cheeses from Spain and Portugal, ranging from tiny disks of fresh cow's milk cheese to wheels of aged sheep's milk. Needless to say, prices are far below any cheese specialty store.

1000 South Elmora Avenue
Elizabeth, NJ 07202
908-355-0700

1132 Liberty Avenue
Hillside, NJ 07205
908-351-5252

64 Pacific Street
Newark, NJ 07105
973-589-8977

260 Lafayette Street
Newark, NJ 07105
973-589-8606

119 Ferry Street
Newark, NJ 07105
973-589-5008

574 Ferry Street
Newark, NJ 07105
973-491-0399

180 Schuyler Avenue
Kearny, NJ 07032
201-998-6545

7:30 A.M. to 9:00 P.M. Monday through Saturday
7:30 A.M. to 8:00 P.M Sunday

## SUBZI MANDI CASH & CARRY
Is bigger better?

Once you've lived in Edison long enough, you'll find yourself ignoring the excitement of its global food resources and instead begin obsessing over minute differences in the price of canned goods. It is at this point that you know you're among the ethnic food shopping hard-core. Yes, looking for the lowest price on basmati rice is like looking for the cheapest gas station. The prices can change while you're shopping, but that's just part of the game.

Subzi Mandi is a great store for both those newly enchanted by the world of Indian food, and those who are so hard-core that they'd drive twenty miles to save five cents a can on mango pulp. It's the biggest grocery store on the Oak Tree Road Indian shopping strip. With a huge parking lot and twice the floor space of its nearest competitor, you can find remarkable variety here.

Subzi Mandi shines with its produce. I spotted fresh chickpeas, baby green mangoes, and nice looking jackfruit in my first few minutes. After that I was lost; I couldn't believe the number of fruits, vegetables, and herbs that I couldn't recognize or had never even heard of.

1538 Oak Tree Road
Iselin, NJ 08830
732-603-0588
9:00 A.M. to 9:00 P.M. 7 days a week

## SUPREMO FOOD MARKET

Supremo markets are well named—they are certainly the supreme source for whatever Latin American ingredients you might need. With groceries and condiments from all over the Caribbean, Central, and South America, this will be your first and last stop for anything from that region you might need.

Look in their produce section. Not only are there the usual items at low prices, you'll also find great looking yucca, *apio* (celeriac or celery ), and *panapen* (breadfruit). In no other store is lard so highly revered. Chilled, but non-hydrogenated, lard is in a case right by the vegetables and tubs and boxes of it in several other forms.

Spices cover a wide range; *puya* and *mulato* are among the lesser known types of chiles available here. *Chia, comino* (cumin), and *annatto* seeds are at the beginning of a long list of other hard-to-find items. The dairy section is just as unique, with over twenty types of fresh cheese including *quesito Colombiano, cotija*, and Oaxaca. *Cremas*, or bottled creams include Centro Americano, Salvadorano, and Mexicana varieties. Even the snack department has Good O West Indian Fruit Soda.

If you fear that the foods at Supremo are too fattening, you have nothing to worry about; they carry Atkins products too.

25 South Broad Street
Elizabeth, NJ 07202
908-351-3399

910–914 Springfield Avenue
Irvington, NJ 07011
973-399-9055

323 Palisades Avenue
Jersey City, NJ 07307
201-963-7606

93–97 Smith Street
Perth Amboy, NJ 08861
732-826-3996

249 East Front Street
Plainfield, NJ 07060
908-668-9855

8:00 A.M. to 9:30 P.M. 7 days a week

## WHOLE EARTH CENTER

Do you think seriously about where your food comes from? Do ideas like "organic" and "fair trade" resonate deeply with you? Then the Whole Earth Center is your store. With a remarkable selection of organic vegetables, fruit, and meats, this is a "heath food" store that sells food that really looks healthy.

The Whole Earth Center also has a large selection of bulk cereals and grains, and a complete cosmetics and household items section. This is the only store in New Jersey where a person can spend hours browsing among different granolas.

When you can't look at another gassed tomato or fluorescent pink steak and the thought of any food created by a scientist instead of a farmer drives you bonkers, a trip to Whole Earth Center will make things right again.

360 Nassau Street (Route 27)
Princeton, NJ 08540
609-924-7429
9:00 A.M. to 8:00 P.M. Monday through Friday
9:00 A.M. to 7:00 P.M. Saturday
10:00 A.M. to 5:00 P.M. Sunday

# RESOURCES

**POINT OF SALE DEFINITIONS:**

**On-site farm store** – A retail shop open year-round.

**On-site farm stand** – Retail stand or store open seasonally.

**CSA** – Membership required, see page 98.

**Market sales** – Sells at regional farmer's markets.

Call ahead for more information.

## WINE

**TOMASELLO WINERY**
225 White Horse Pike
Hammonton, NJ 08037
800-MMM-WINE
www.tomasellowinery.com
On-site farm store and catering facility

**BELLVIEW WINERY**
150 Atlantic Street
Landisville, NJ 08326
856-697-7172
www.bellviewwinery.com
On-site farm store

**BOBOLINK DAIRY**
42 Meadow Burn Road
Vernon, NJ 07462
973-764-4888
www.cowsoutside.com
On-site farm store, market sales

**FARMERSVILLE CHEESES**
Valley Shepherd Creamery
Route 517 (Fairmount Rd) at the corner of Route 513
Long Valley, NJ 07853
908-832-7088
www.farmersvillecheeses.com
www.valleyshepherd.com
on-site farm store, market sales

**STONEY CROFT FARM**
163 Beaver Run Road
Lafayette, NJ 07848
973-875-5611
On-site farm store, market sales

## FISH

**STEWART TWEED OYSTER FARM**
Green Creek, NJ
609-886-6573
No retail sales

**MUSKY TROUT HATCHERY**
279 Bloomsbury Road, Asbury, NJ 08802
908-638-8747
On-site farm market

## POULTRY AND EGGS

**KELLER FARM**
601 Moss Mill Road, Germania,
(Egg Harbor City) NJ 08215
609-965-5165
On-site farm market, market sales

### GRIGGSTOWN QUAIL FARM
986 Canal Road, Princeton, NJ 08540
908-359-5375
www.griggstownquailfarm.com
On-site farm store

### ABMA'S FARM MARKET
700 Lawlins Road
Wyckoff, NJ 07481
201-891-0278
www.abmasfarm.com
On-site farm store

### FLATBROOK FARM
2 DeGroat Road
Montague (Sandyston Township), NJ 07827
973-948-2554
On-site farm store

## MEAT
### NEPTUNE FARM
723 Harmersville-
Canton Road
Salem, NJ 08079
856-935-3612
www.neptunefarm.com
No retail sales

### READINGTON RIVER BUFFALO COMPANY
937 Route 523
Readington Township (Flemington), NJ 08822
908-806-0030
www.thebuffalofarm.com
On-site farm store

### SIMPLY GRAZIN' FARM
182 Vandyke Road
Hopewell, NJ 08525
609-466-8504
sforganic.com
On-site farm stand

## VEGETABLES AND FRUIT
### ASBURY'S NATURAL VILLAGE FARM
Route 643, Main Street
Asbury, NJ 08802
908-537-2846
www.asburyfarm.org
CSA

### SPRINGHILL FARM
Hopewell, NJ
609-466-4747
Market sales

### RACE FARM
87 Belcher Road
Blairstown, NJ 07825
908-362-8151
www.racefarm.com
On-site market stand,
market sales

### THE PHILLY CHILE COMPANY
Monroeville, NJ
856-358-1431
www.phillychile.com
Market sales

### OAK SHADE FARM
Denville, NJ
Aaaalex@yahoo.com
Market sales

### UPPER MEADOWS FARM
16 Pollara Lane
Montague, NJ 07827
973-293-8171
www.uppermeadowsfarm.com
CSA, market sales

### CHIA-SIN FARMS
215 Quakertown Road
Pittstown, NJ 08867
908-730-7123
On-site farm stand, pick-your-own

218

## STOKES FARM
Old Tappan, NJ
201-768-3931
Market sales

## WELL-SWEEP HERB FARM
205 Mount Bethel Road
Port Murray, NJ 07865
908-852-5390
www.wellsweep.com
On-site farm store

## WATERSHED ORGANIC FARM
260 Wargo Road,
Hopewell Township
(Pennington), NJ
08534
609-737-8899
www.watershedfarm.com
CSA

## E.R. & SON FARM
572 Buckleview Avenue
Monroe Township, NJ 08831
732-521-2591
On-site farm store

## J.C. HAZLETT FARM AND MARKET
570 Route 47 North
Goshen, NJ 08210
609-861-5551
Market sales

## FOX'S CRANBERRIES
5741 Cranberry Court
Weekstown, NJ 08215
609-965-0358

## PEACEFUL VALLEY ORCHARDS
441 Pittstown Road (Route 615)
Pittstown, NJ 08867
908-713-1705
www.peacefulvalleyorchards.com
On-site farm stand, market sales

## TERHUNE ORCHARDS
330 Cold Soil Road
Princeton, NJ 08540
609-924-2310
www.terhuneorchards.com
On-site farm store, market sales

## BIG BUCK FARMS
Hammonton, NJ
609-965-5604
No retail sales

### NORTHEAST ORGANIC FARMING

Association of New Jersey (NOFA-NJ)
60 S. Main St., P.O. Box 886
Pennington, NJ 08334
609-737-6848 (phone), 609-737-2366 (fax)
www.nofanj.org

### NEW JERSEY COUNCIL OF FARMERS AND COMMUNITIES - NJCFC

P.O. Box 1114
Madison, New Jersey 07940-1114
973-236-1875 (phone/fax)
www.njcfc.org
info@njcfc.org

### JERSEY FRESH RETAIL INFORMATION

New Jersey Department of Agriculture –
Division of Markets
P.O. Box 330
Trenton, New Jersey 08625
609-292-0170
www.state.nj.us/jerseyfresh/index.html

### NEW JERSEY MUSEUM OF AGRICULTURE

PO Box 7788
North Brunswick, NJ 08902
103 College Farm Rd
North Brunswick, NJ 08902
732-249-2077
www.agriculturemuseum.org
info@agriculturemuseum.org

220

# BIBLIOGRAPHY

Brody, Helen. *New Hampshire: From Farm to Kitchen*. New York: Hippocrene Books, 2004.

Goria, Giovanni. *La Cucina Del Piemonte*. Padova (MI) Italy: Franco Muzzio Editore, 1990.

Purdy, Susan G. *As Easy As Pie*. New York: Atheneum, 1984.

Robbins, Maria Polushkin. *The Dumpling Cookbook*. New York: Workman Publishing, 1977.

Rombauer, Irma S. and Marion Rombauer Becker. *The Joy of Cooking*. New York: Scribner, 1995.

Salatin, Joel. *Family Friendly Farming: A Multi-Generational Home-Based Business Testament*. White River Junction, VT: Chelsea Green Publishers, 2001.

Simonds, Nina. *Classic Chinese Cuisine*. Boston: Houghton Mifflin Company, 1982.

Slow Food Editore. *Ricette delle Osterie di Langa*. Bra (CN), Italy: Arcigola Slow Food Editore, 1992.

# INDEX

**N O T E :** Page numbers in **bold** distinguish general information from recipes.

226

**228**

# Other Hippocrene Cookbooks from the Americas

## Aprovecho
A Mexican-American Border Cookbook
*Teresa Cordero-Cordell and Robert Cordell*

This cookbook is a celebration of the food and culture found along the U.S.-Mexico border. Aprovecho contains traditional fare including enchiladas, quesadillas, and margaritas, along with more exotic delights, such as Cactus Salad (*Ensalada de Nopalitos*), Lobster and Tequila (*Langosta y Tequila*), and Watermelon Sorbet. The recipes included feature a tantalizing array of ingredients from both sides of the Border. Easy-to-follow instructions will have you creating Border delights in no time!
377 pages • 6 x 9 • 0 7818 1026 4 • W • $24.95HC • (22)

## Cooking with Cajun Women
Recipes and Remembrances from South Louisiana Kitchens
*Nicole Fontenot*

In this treasury of Cajun heritage, the author allows the people who were the very foundations of Cajun culture to tell their own stories. She visited Cajun women in their homes and kitchens  and gathered more than 300 recipes as well as thousands of narrative accounts. Most of these women were raised on small farms and remember a time when almost everything was homemade. They share traditional recipes updated with modern ingredients. This cookbook enables its users to recreate such typical Cajun wonders as Crawfish Etouffée, Sausage Rice Jambalaya, Fig Cakes, Gumbo, and Pralines.
380 pages • 6 x 9 • 0 7818 0932 0 • W • $24.95HC • (75)

## New Hampshire
From Farm to Kitchen
*Helen Brody*

A comprehensive look at New Hampshire's rich store of gastronomic treasures including profiles of some of the Granite State's most important working farms. Quick and easy recipes, using each farm's raw ingredients, make the direct, and often overlooked, connection between the farmer who grows the food and the cook who prepares it. The author also offers menus for traditional state events and a resource section that will enable readers and cooks to locate the farms and their products.
285 pages • 7 x 10 • 0-7818-1021-3 • $18.95pb • (561)

## A Taste of Haiti
*Mirta Yurnet*

With African, French, Arabic and Amerindian influences, the food and culture of Haiti are fascinating subjects to explore. From the days of slavery to present times, traditional Haitian cuisine has relied upon staples such as root vegetables, pork, fish, and flavor enhancers like *Pikliz* (picklese or, hot pepper vinegar) and *Zepis* (ground spices). This cookbook presents more than 100 traditional Haitian recipes, which are complemented by information on Haiti's history, holidays and celebrations, necessary food staples, and cooking methods. Recipe titles are presented in English, Creole, and French.

180 pages • 5½ x 8½ • 0 7818 0927 4 • W • $24.95HC • (8)

## A Taste of Quebec (Second Edition)
*Julian Armstrong*

First published in 1990, *A Taste of Quebec* is the definitive guide to traditional and modern cooking in this distinctive region of Canada. Now revised and updated, the second edition features over 125 new recipes and traditional favorites, along with highlights on up-and-coming new chefs, the province's best restaurants, notes of architectural and historical interest, and typical regional menus for a genuine Quebecois feast. With photos illustrating the people, the cuisine, and the land sprinkled throughout, this is *the* food lover's guide to Quebec.

200 pages • 8-page color insert • 7¾ x 9⅜ • 0-7818-0902-9 • $16.95pb • (32)

Prices subject to change without prior notice. To purchase Hippocrene books contact your local bookstore, call (718) 454-2366, visit www.hippocrenebooks.com, or write to: HIPPOCRENE BOOKS, Madison Avenue, New York, NY 10016. Please enclose check or money order, adding $5.00 shipping and handling (UPS) for the first book and $.50 for each additional book.